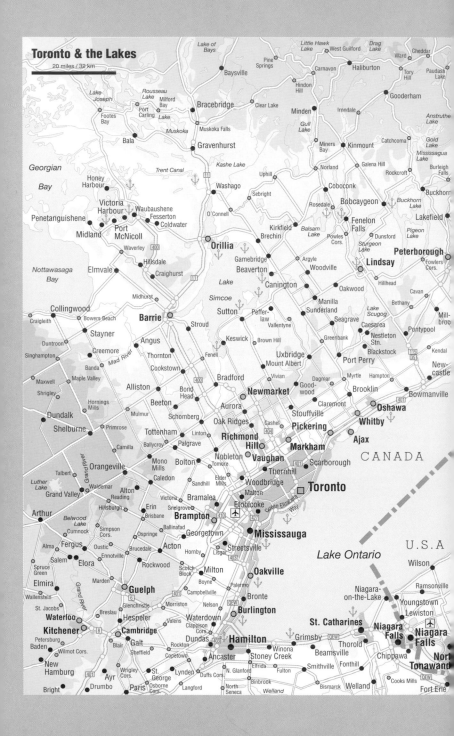

Toronto & the Lakes

20 miles / 32 km

INSIGHT POCKET GUIDE

TORONTO

Discovery CHANNEL

APA PUBLICATIONS
Part of the Langenscheidt Publishing Group

Welcome!

This guidebook combines the interests and enthusiasms of two of the world's best-known information providers: Insight Guides, who have set the standard for visual travel guides since 1970, and Discovery Channel, the world's premier source of non-fiction television programming.

Toronto is a city rich in museums and theatres, ethnic neighbourhoods and international cuisine, and one that has beaches and islands on its doorstep. It has been described as 'the most hopeful and healthy city in North America' – which sums up the local spirit that we hope you will discover for yourself. In the following pages our correspondent offers detailed itineraries to help make things even easier and to ensure that you get the most out of a brief stay. Most of the suggested routes concentrate on the city itself, but an excursion to Niagara Falls, a priority with many visitors to Canada, could not be left out.

Joanna Ebbutt is a travel writer and editor, and a long-time Toronto resident. During her time living in Canada she has not only written about Toronto, but also guided countless friends, relatives and acquaintances through the nuances of city life. She is looking forward to sharing the delights of her adopted city with you, acquainting you with its colourful past and offering the kind of practical tips and inside information that will help to make your stay a real pleasure.

C O N T E N T S

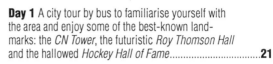

Excursions

Shopping, Dining & Nightlife

Calendar of Events

Practical Information

Maps

Pages 8/9: Past and present

HISTORY &

In The Beginning

First Nations tribes first settled in the Toronto area around 1000BC, but it was not until Samuel de Champlain, the governor of New France, sent an explorer called Etienne Brûlé to investigate the area in 1615, that the Iroquois village of Teiaiagon was discovered on the east bank of the Humber River. Towards the end of the century, Toronto first appeared on maps, and seemed to cover an extensive part of southern Ontario. The name originated from a Huron word meaning 'Place of Meeting'.

Over the years, the French gradually established themselves – at that time most of southern Québec and southern Ontario was called Québec – and in 1720 they built a fur trading post to do business with the local Mississauga tribe, who by then had replaced the Iroquois. Thirty years later they built Fort Rouillé, on what is now Toronto's Canadian National Exhibition grounds.

With the defeat of the French at the Battle of the Plains of Abraham in 1759, the British became the power-brokers of the Great Lakes region, and in 1787 purchased the land on which Toronto now stands from the Mississauga, in exchange for £1,700 in cash, augmented by goods such as flannel, axes and food.

Trade with the locals

Culture

Slowly a settlement grew up around the natural harbour, and in 1790 the construction of Yonge Street commenced, to replace the old canoe route from Lake Ontario to Lake Huron — a simple beginning for what is now the world's longest street, extending 1,900km (1,181 miles) from Lake Ontario to Rainy River, in northern Ontario.

Traditional hunting methods

Québec was divided into two colonies in 1791 — Lower Canada (today's southern Québec) and Upper Canada (today's southern Ontario). Initially Niagara-on-the-Lake was the capital of Upper Canada, but in 1793 Toronto was renamed York (a tribute to George III's son, the Duke of York) and established as the new capital by Lieutenant-Colonel John Graves Simcoe, governor of Upper Canada. York was chosen because of the potential its harbour offered as a naval station, and its distance from the troublesome Americans. One of the first bills passed by Simcoe's Assembly was to abolish slavery — four decades before it was declared illegal in the rest of the British Empire, and almost 75 years before the United States followed suit.

During the War of 1812, the 700-strong population of York remained loyal to Britain, although the town was occupied twice, albeit briefly, by the Americans in 1813. Today, only the military grid system of streets remains as evidence of Simcoe's times.

One of Toronto's many names, Muddy York, originated during the early 1800s, a comment on the state of the roads at that time. Edward Allen Talbot, a British colonist, described Toronto in 1824 as 'better calculated for a frog pond or a beaver meadow than for the residence of human beings'. Nonetheless, British immigrants were arriving thick and fast. By 1834 the population had increased to 9,252. The first Jewish immigrants began arriving in 1830, mostly from England, Germany and the US. The seeds of Toronto's later cosmopolitan status were already being sown.

City Expansion

The size and economic stature of York led to it being incorporated as a city in 1834, and renamed Toronto. Socio-economic divisions inevitably occurred, and the old guard, mostly Tories, were constantly being challenged by reform-minded citizens. One result was the disastrously organised Upper Canadian Rebellion in December 1837, instigated by Toronto's first mayor, William Lyon Mackenzie. Due to bad communications and hopeless organisation the rebellion failed; fortunately there were few casualties, and life in Toronto soon resumed its normal pace.

Upper and Lower Canada were replaced by the new United Province in 1841, and the capital rotated – in a somewhat unsatisfactory arrangement – between Toronto and Québec City, until Queen Victoria selected Ottawa as Canada's permanent capital in 1865.

In the meantime, the city continued to grow, and the University of Toronto opened its doors in 1843. Forty thousand Irish immigrants landed in Toronto, driven from their homeland by hunger as a result of the potato famine in 1847. Some continued out west, but many stayed. Despite the first of two great fires, there was a boom in communications generally, through the growth of railways, roads, canals, shipping and telegraph lines during the 1850s. But the city wasn't all about work: baseball made its first appearance in the 1850s, and rowing and horse racing became extremely popular. St Lawrence Hall (Toronto's City Hall at that time) hosted not only major political meetings, but world-renowned entertainers such as Jenny Lind and Tom Thumb.

All this activity culminated in Toronto becoming the capital of the newly created province of Ontario, upon the confederation of Canada in 1867. By 1879 it had its first telephone exchange, with 40 subscribers. The same year, Sir Sandford Fleming invented the concept of Standard Time, while working at the University of Toronto.

Parliament Building

Sign of success

The population grew un-abated, as Toronto continued to receive Welsh, German and Irish Catholic immigrants – driven from their homes by poverty – as well as blacks fleeing from slavery in the United States. More Jewish settlers arrived in the 1880s after the massive upheavals in Russia.

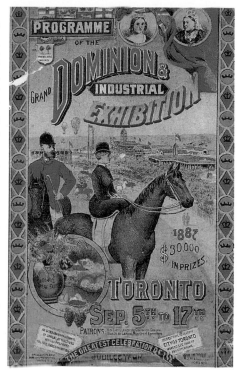

'Toronto The Good'

Towards the end of the 19th century, Toronto earned an-other of its sobriquets. Its loyalty to Queen Victoria and the British Empire, and its firm belief in the sanctity of the Sabbath, lead to its rep-utation as 'Toronto the Good'. This reputation was solidified by the federally imposed Lord's Day legislation, which prohibited most working, sporting and entertainment activities on Sunday. To this day, Toronto is working hard to shake off that worthy reputation.

There was a spate of designing public buildings, such as Old City Hall and Queen's Park, the provincial legislature, in a massive, ornate Romanesque style, entirely reflecting the belief of Toronto's upper echelons in the natural order of life. But even for the masses, life was improving. Central heating, hot water and indoor plumbing became standard in many homes, and other developments such as the automobile, electricity and high rise buildings began to have an immense impact.

And still the immigrants arrived. Between 1900 and 1911, up to 1½ million people came to Canada, from south and east Europe and from Britain. As with the earlier influx, some went west, but many settled in Montréal and Toronto.

At the same time, the arts were attaining ever-increasing support. The period between 1908 and 1915 saw the establishment of the Toronto Symphony Orchestra, the Art Gallery of Ontario and the Royal Ontario Museum. In the science arena, Dr Frederick Banting's discovery of insulin (for which he was awarded the Nobel Prize), while at the University of Toronto, once again put the city on the world stage.

There were few bright spots during the Great Depression of the 1930s. Historic St Lawrence Hall was used as a flop house for several years, and Canadian unemployment reached a horrendous 32 percent. Extremes of weather seemed to match the economic hardships: winters can be bitterly cold, but during a July heat wave

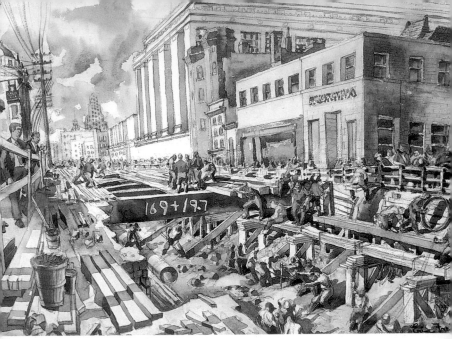

Building Toronto's subway

in 1936, one wit fried an egg on the steps of City Hall. During World War II, there was a burgeoning of economic activity as the country supported the war effort.

After World War II, Toronto the Good's reputation began to show some cracks. In 1947, the first cocktail bars were allowed, despite the howling of outraged critics. A massive increase in the population of Toronto and surrounding areas, caused by fresh waves of immigrants from Europe, resulted, in 1953, in the amalgamation of the city of Toronto with surrounding townships, to become the Municipality of Metropolitan Toronto. The badly needed subway finally opened in 1954, connecting Union Station to Eglinton Avenue and reducing traffic congestion.

As another sign of the changing times, Nathan Phillips – the man who spearheaded the building of New City Hall – was elected Toronto's first Jewish mayor, in 1955. Another step on the road to liberalisation and cultural freedom took place in the 1960s, when Torontonians were finally allowed to go to movies, plays and concerts on Sundays. It was also said to be in the name of progress when developers began to tear down everything that stood in the way of their new constructions, but they were met with determined opposition. Battle lines were quickly drawn and although there were some losses, buildings such as Old City Hall, Union Station, Holy Trinity Church and many others were saved from destruction.

Flower-powered youth moved into Yorkville in the late 1960s, squatting in the old and somewhat derelict Victorian homes. In a few years, however, they were ousted, and the buildings were tastefully restored. Ironically, Yorkville is now everything that the flower-children would have rejected, packed with trendy boutiques, galleries and chic restaurants.

Contemporary Toronto

The last 25 years have seen the city change dramatically. The path was set by the election as mayor, in 1972, of David Crombie. A Conservative reformer, he played a significant role in making the city as livable as it now is. Height limits were set on new buildings, and many century-old houses were renovated in previously poor immigrant areas, such as Cabbagetown. However, this did not create affordable accommodation and subsidised housing in new downtown developments began to appear. Areas such as the St Lawrence Market acquired fresh vitality as a direct result of such developments, which included a healthy mixture of socio-economic groupings.

Cabbagetown's Victorian dwellings

Unlike many North American cities, Toronto has a vibrant inner core. The downtown population grew by almost four percent between 1986 and 1991, and although there are poor neighbourhoods, there are no ghettos, and the crime rate is much lower than in any comparable North American city. In 1989, only 500 parking spaces were installed at SkyDome (later renamed Rogers Centre) – the new downtown home for Toronto's baseball and football teams – deliberately encouraging people to use the city's public transport system and downtown streets.

The mass evacuation of businesses, and Anglo-Québecers generally, from Montréal to Toronto, precipitated by French nationalism and the election of the separatist provincial government in 1976, also had a major impact on the growth of Toronto's downtown core. Bilingual street signs began to appear in many of Toronto's ethnic neighbourhoods. The relaxation of federal immigration laws also resulted in the arrival of people from Africa, Asia, Latin America and the Caribbean.

The 1970s and 1980s saw the addition of several major structures that had further impact on the local and global scene, starting with the CN Tower – at 553m (1,815ft) the world's tallest unsupported structure, and Toronto's most recognisable symbol. In 1979, the Eaton Centre was completed, a $200 million, 6-hectare (15-acre) development, with 302 stores on four levels, and 10 years later came SkyDome. In 1999 came the completion of the Air Canada Centre, where the titans of professional

The CN Tower

Skyscrapers and sails

ice hockey and basketball hold sway. All four entertain and thrill thousands of visitors, year after year, and make a palpable difference to the city's coffers.

There is also a huge creative community – the diversity of Toronto's cultural sector is reflected in newspapers such as *Now* and *Eye*, where there are pages listing theatre and literary events, concerts and new gallery showings. In tandem with this, Toronto has become a major centre for film-making, including high-tech animation.

The influence of more than 80 different ethnic groups, on a total population of 2.5 million in Toronto (5 million in the Greater Toronto Area), is immeasurable. Certain signs are obvious, such as the myriad restaurants producing world cuisine, but the overall psyche of so many different peoples living together in one city is not easy to measure. How do you gauge acceptance and understanding? The numbers are awesome – over 259,000 Chinese, 254,000 South Asian, 204,000 black, 138,700 Italian, 86,500 Filipino and 75,800 Portuguese. During the week-long Caribbean Caribana festival, non-stop music pounds away and photos of dancers tucking into curried goat, hot Jamaican patties and pots of chicken at the Toronto Islands picnic fill local papers. The days when most Torontonians had British ancestry are long gone. Visitors to Toronto should try a *gelato* in Little Italy, *dim-sum* in Chinatown, or *souvlaki* on the Danforth to appreciate the city's splendid variety of cultures.

The election of mayor, David Miller, in 2003, heralded a new era. A grassroots guy, Miller travels by public transport and is committed to Toronto remaining one of the world's most liveable big cities. Ambitious plans for the area include the restoration of the city's waterfront and in the year that Miller was elected the Distillery Historic District opened with great fanfare. Originally founded in 1832 on 5 hectares (13 acres) downtown, it houses art galleries, ateliers, a microbrewery, restaurants, bars and performance space. The pedestrian-only village is a favourite of Torontonians and visitors alike.

Playground pleasures

Historical Highlights

Pre 1600s Entire region inhabited by First Nations.

1615 Etienne Brûlé, a French explorer, discovers the village of the Teiaiagon tribe , on the site of what is now Toronto.

1720 The French set up a fur trading post in order to trade with Mississauga nation.

1750 France builds Fort Rouillé.

1759 Defeat of French in the Battle of the Plains of Abraham in Québec City led to British becoming the main power in the Great Lakes region.

1787 The Mississauga nation sell the land on which Toronto now stands to the English.

1793 Town of York is made the capital of the recently formed Upper Canada, by its governor, Lieutenant-Colonel John Graves Simcoe.

1812 War of 1812.

1813 York is occupied twice, briefly, by Americans.

1834 York is elevated to city status and renamed Toronto.

1837 Upper Canadian Rebellion instigated by Major William Lyon Mackenzie fails.

1841 Upper and Lower Canada are reorganised as the United Province.

1843 University of Toronto opens.

1847 40,000 Irish refugees arrive in Toronto, as a result of the potato famine.

1867 Toronto becomes capital of the newly created province of Ontario within the confederation of Canada.

1879 Sir Sandford Fleming invents Standard Time at the University of Toronto.

1906 The reputation of 'Toronto the Good' is solidified by the Lord's Day legislation prohibiting most work, sport and entertainment on Sunday.

1921 Discovery of insulin by Dr Frederick Banting, while working at the University of Toronto.

1929 Black Thursday on 24 October heralds the arrival of the Great Depression.

1931 Maple Leaf Gardens opens, a 12,586-seat ice hockey arena.

1939 War brought close to home when a German torpedo destroys the liner *Athenia*, killing all passengers, including 200 Toronto citizens.

1947 The first cocktail bars are allowed in Toronto.

1954 Hurricane Hazel causes damage valued at $25 million, and the death of 81 people. Subway opens, connecting Union Station with Eglinton Avenue.

1970s Mass evacuation of Anglo-Québecers from Montréal to Toronto.

1972 Election of David Crombie as Mayor of Toronto, a Conservative who plays a major role in reforming the city.

1978 Election of John Sewell as Mayor, a radical reformer who continued Crombie's policies.

1993 The inauguration of the Princess of Wales Theatre, as well as the North York Performing Art Centre, further enriches the city's cultural life.

1998 The City of Toronto is amalgamated with five neighbouring municipalities creating a 'megacity'; an unpopular move that instigated demands for the formation of a new province of Toronto.

1999 Air Canada Centre opens, it becomes home to the Maple Leafs and the Toronto Raptors.

2003 The Distillery Historic District opens. David Miller is elected mayor, he promises a new waterfront area and a corruption-free city hall.

2005 The provincial government unveils plans for a green belt around the Greater Toronto Area – from Niagara Falls to Peterborough, north of the city.

Toronto

400 m / 440 yards

Day Itiner

Most of the explorations described in this book focus on the central core of the city that became an amalgamation of six municipalities on 1 January 1998. Days 1–3 have been arranged to give you an overall flavour of the city, while the Pick & Mix section allows you to create your own itinerary. For the excursion to Niagara, aim for an early start.

The TTC Rocket

One of the reasons why visitors enjoy Toronto so much is that it's an uncomplicated city to get around, based on a north–south, east–west grid. From most of the downtown core you can see one of Toronto's most famous landmarks, the CN Tower. It's close to Lake Ontario – the city's southern border – so unless you've lost all sense of direction, you can work out where you are.

Toronto's public transport system is operated by the Toronto Transit Commission – the TTC – and all the itineraries described here are geared towards a combination of walking and using public transport. The subways are clean, safe and efficient, and since parking downtown can be expensive and difficult, travelling by TTC is often the better way to go – to use their own slogan. (For details on special tickets and passes, *see Practical Information pages 80–89*.) Remember that you need a ticket, token or the exact change for riding on buses and street cars, as drivers don't carry change.

You need not worry about travelling around Toronto alone. Nowhere mentioned in this guide should give cause for concern. If some other areas interest you, check with your hosts or your hotel. Taxis are usually easily found, and fares are reasonable.

Toronto Sights

Breakfast at Richtree Market Restaurant before taking a two-hour sightseeing tour of the city, followed by a walk and lunch in part of the theatre district. Nearby, the CN Tower provides an aerial perspective to the morning tour. Finish up with an early evening cocktail at the top of the tower or afternoon tea at one of Toronto's most famous hotels, the Royal York Hotel.

–To the start: although Gray Line Tours pick up passengers from many downtown hotels, breakfast at Richtree is a fun, energising way to begin your first day in Toronto. Take the TTC to King Street subway station. Exit at Yonge Street, southwest corner and walk south. Shortly after you have crossed Wellington Street, you come to the entrance of BCE Place. Prices (per person) for the main sights are indicated as follows: $ = under $10; $$ = under $20; $$$ = under $30. All prices given in this guide are in Canadian dollars. Enjoy!–

In a metropolis the size of Toronto, a general sightseeing tour is an excellent way to get a 'fix' on the city. Gray Line Tours (tel: 416-594-3310; www.grayline.com) operate throughout the year with a Hop-On/Hop-Off city tour. You may either remain on board a trolley, or – in the summer – an open-air double-decker bus for the two-hour fully narrated tour, or hop off and on at any of the stops along the route. While we suggest you lunch downtown, you may alight in Yorkville to browse and lunch there, before continuing the journey. The service begins at 9am and runs every 20 minutes

Richtree Market Restaurant

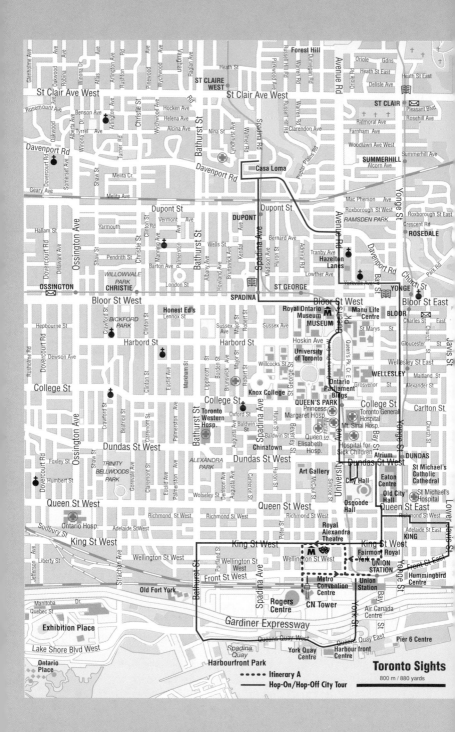

Toronto Sights

800 m / 880 yards

- - - - Itinerary A
━━━ Hop-On/Hop-Off City Tour

The Royal York Hotel

during peak summer season. Tickets ($$$) are valid for two days and can be purchased from your hotel or on board the tour bus.

Begin your day with a relaxing breakfast around 8am at Richtree Market Restaurant, in **BCE Place** – designed by Spanish architect Santiago Calatrava, it is one of Toronto's most magnificent downtown developments. From Yonge Street you enter **Heritage Square**, where gaily coloured banners adorn the exterior of the restaurant. Inside, you'll be faced with a buffet-style selection of muesli, croissants, muffins and generously-sized omelettes, pancakes, and waffles. Afterwards, leave BCE Place through the **Galleria**, where a soaring cathedral-styled lobby is flooded with dappled lighting.

Hockey enthusiasts may like to make the most of their proximity to the **Hockey Hall of Fame** (tel: 416-360-7765; www.hhof.com) to pay a visit, although be warned it doesn't open until 10am. It can be reached by taking the escalator down to the concourse level. There are 17 different exhibits with interactive displays and games where you can sit in an announcer's booth calling the play-by-play of famous goals, try to stop Wayne Gretzky's shots as soft rubber pucks fly at you from a virtual reality screen or shoot pucks against a life-sized, computer-simulated Eddie 'The Eagle' Belfour. Hallowed objects such as the Stanley Cup – including the original Stanley Cup bowl donated by Lord Stanley of Preston in 1882 – are housed in Great Hall.

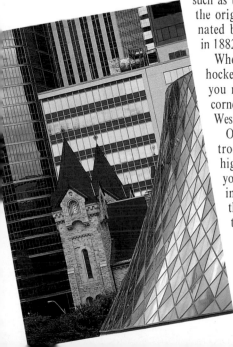

Whether you opt to visit this hockey shrine or not, ultimately you must head to the southeast corner of Yonge and Front Street West to join the sightseeing tour.

On the tour, you will be introduced to many of Toronto's highlights, a number of which you will return to, and explore in more detail later. Along the way, you'll receive a potted, anecdotal history of the city and the many and diverse people who have made it their home over the past 200 years.

St Andrew's Church

Roy Thomson Hall

At the end of the tour, get off at the **Royal York Hotel**. It has been a Toronto landmark since 1929, with its green copper, château-style roof. Built by Canadian Pacific Railways, it was, at the time of its construction, the greatest and the tallest hotel in the British Empire. Walk north up York Street one block to King Street West and turn left. Cross over University Avenue and continue west. At the southeast corner of King Street and Simcoe is **St Andrew's Presbyterian Church**. On a sunny day the walls of the **Sun Life Centre** on the opposite side of the road present a dazzling juxtaposition of old and new, with the church, Roy Thomson Hall and the CN Tower reflected in the glass. When the church was built in 1876, the other three corners were occupied by Government House, Upper Canada College (a prestigious boys' school that later moved to another location) and a popular tavern. For a while the corner was known as Legislation, Education, Damnation and Salvation.

Royal Alexandra Theatre

On the other side of Simcoe Street, **Roy Thomson Hall** (www.roythomson.com) is Toronto's main concert hall – a futuristic-looking building designed by Canadian architect Arthur Erickson. The shining exterior of honeycombed glass encloses a stunningly airy lobby, which in turn encircles the concert hall with its state-of-the-art acoustics. It is named after billionaire news-paper magnate Lord Thomson of Fleet, whose family gave the largest single donation towards its construction. Volunteers lead occasional 60- or 90-minute tours of the 2,600-seat auditorium for a small fee and function rooms are available to rent.

Now cross to the north side of King Street. The next two blocks, from Simcoe Street West to John Street, are home to two magnificent theatres. Both are the result of the 40-year-long efforts of one man, Ed Mirvish, and later his son, David.

Book-ended by the theatres are a number of restaurants and watering holes such as Quotes Bar and Grill, the Elephant & Castle Pub, Big Daddy's Crab Shack & Oyster Bar, Kama Classical Indian Cuisine and King's Garden Chinese Cuisine.

Ed Mirvish's career started with the opening of Honest Ed's *(see Shopping, pages 66–68)* in the 1940s, but he entered the theatrical business with the acquisition in 1962 of the historical **Royal Alexandra Theatre**. Built in 1907, it seemed destined to become another downtown car park but was rescued by Ed Mirvish, who spent huge sums of money on restoring the building to its original Edwardian splendour before bringing in the hundreds of first-rate productions which have been staged over the last 30 years. In fact, many of the greatest actors in the English-speaking world have performed on the Alexandra's stage.

In 1993, Mirvish and his son David opened their third theatre, the **Princess of Wales**, at the corner of King and John streets. It was built specifically to accommodate the hit musical *Miss Saigon*, and it continues to host one blockbuster after another, such as the world premiere of a musical adaptation of *The Lord of the Rings* in 2006.

At John Street, head south towards the **CN Tower** (Sun–Thur 9.30am–10pm, Fri–Sat until 10.30pm; www.cntower.ca) – it's barely a five-minute walk and, at 553m (1,815ft), or 181 storeys, you certainly can't miss it. In case of inclement weather, such as low cloud, post-pone your trip. Instead, walk to nearby **Rogers Centre** – see *Pick & Mix Option 3* – or visit **Theatre Q's** (322 King Street West), one door west of the Princess of Wales Theatre. Down in the basement is Toronto's only shop devoted to theatre memorabilia, and merchandise from current shows.

Once at the Tower, purchase tickets ($$) at the base. There's plenty to see and do at the bottom of the tower, including various interactive arcade games and attractions. Drop by the Maple Leaf cinema to watch a fascinating 15-minute video on the building of the tower, including dramatic footage of the bright orange Sikorsky helicopter installing the final section of the

Mirvish Territory

CN Tower

102m (335ft) antenna one Sunday morning in March 1975.

In fact, the primary purpose of the tower is communications – currently more than 30 Toronto radio and TV stations transmit to southern Ontario. Summer weekends are busiest, when the longest waits are between 11am–5pm. Reservations to **360 Restaurant** (tel: 416-362-5411) include a fast track ride up; you can visit the observation levels before or after your meal. On windy days, the lifts are automatically slowed down by roof-top sensors but normally it takes 58 seconds, in external lifts with floor-to-ceiling glass doors, to reach the first of three observation levels – the Look Out Level at 346m (1,136ft), where you will find **Horizons**, the world's highest café and bar, ideal for a drink at sunset.

To reach the lowest level of the tower you will need to descend a flight of stairs after exiting the lift, for the outside observation deck and Glass Floor Level, where you can stand on almost 24 sq m (256 sq ft) of solid glass, with the world 342m (1,122ft) below.

For a couple of dollars more, you can take another lift up to the Sky Pod – at 147 storeys or 447m (1,465ft), it's the highest public observation gallery in the world. You may feel the subtle movement of the tower – don't be alarmed, as the (slight) flexibility increases the strength of the structure. On clear days you can reportedly see up to 160km (100 miles), while below, tiny planes take off and land at Toronto Island Airport and toy street cars trundle along King Street. Even Torontonians who have seen them many times before find the views mesmerising. Afterwards, take the lift down and return to Front Street. Turn right and head towards the subway, only five minutes' walk away. When you come to the Royal York Hotel, consider an afternoon tea of wafer thin sandwiches and scones with cream and jam, in the EPIC restaurant.

Union Station

Otherwise, continue along Front Street to **Union Station**. Built in 1924 in neoclassical style, the vaulted ceiling of the cavernous ticket hall is based on the baths of Imperial Rome, and early Christian basilicas. Some 18m (60ft) above hang the destinations of trans-continental trains, engraved in giant letters. Union Station has witnessed much of Canada's history, and is still the main station for cross country and local commuter trains, and a subway station.

DAY 2

Exploring Downtown and Harbourfront

Breakfast in Trinity Square beside the Toronto Eaton Centre, before a walking tour of downtown's financial district and the historic St Lawrence Market area. After lunch, proceed down to Harbourfront for an afternoon beside the water.

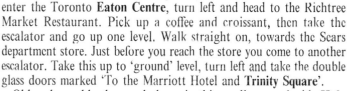

The Eaton Centre

—To the start: take the TTC to Queen Street station, and leave from Albert Street exit at the north end of the platform. This brings you into the food concourse at the Toronto Eaton Centre.—

Today you will need comfortable shoes, although there will be plenty of opportunities to snack, browse or shop. As you enter the Toronto **Eaton Centre**, turn left and head to the Richtree Market Restaurant. Pick up a coffee and croissant, then take the escalator and go up one level. Walk straight on, towards the Sears department store. Just before you reach the store you come to another escalator. Take this up to 'ground' level, turn left and take the double glass doors marked 'To the Marriott Hotel and **Trinity Square**'.

Old and new blend serenely here, in this small square beside **Holy Trinity Church**. Pick a bench and savour both your coffee and the surroundings. The church was built in 1847, and is now surrounded by the Toronto Eaton Centre and a galaxy of shiny new office towers. But you can still hear the birds and be soothed by sounds from the nearby fountain. Two rather whimsical bronze sculptures, *Encounter* and *Neighbours*, add their own somewhat surreal contribution to the square.

The first plans for the Eaton Centre included the demolition of Old City Hall and Holy Trinity Church.

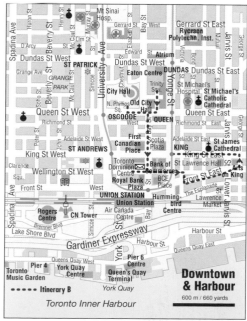

Downtown & Harbour

600 m / 660 yards

- - - - Itinerary B

Toronto Inner Harbour

City Hall and Nathan Phillips Square

Fortunately the uproar that followed the announcement ensured that the plans were overturned. The redesigned Eaton Centre was finally completed in 1979 – a lofty glass palace that unashamedly exposes its pipes, columns and mechanical systems to the world. When you're shopping, look up at the sculpture *Flight Stop* (representing Canada geese in flight), by Canadian artist Michael Snow.

Art deco doors

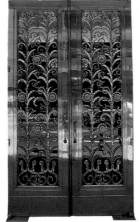

After their installation, he successfully challenged an ill-advised decision by management to drape the geese with Christmas decorations.

Walk south down James Street (which runs beside the Eaton Centre), cross Salvation Army Square and continue to Queen Street West. To your right is the stately **Old City Hall**, with an intricately detailed frieze on the front facade (including caricatures of councillors who had annoyed the architect, E J Lennox). Built in the 1890s, this was Toronto's third city hall.

Cross Bay Street to **Nathan Phillips Square** and **City Hall**, designed by Finnish architect Viljo Revell – the winner of a competition in which 520 architects from 44 countries submitted plans for this 3.5-hectare (9-acre) public area. In summer Nathan Phillips Square (named after Toronto's first Jewish mayor) fairly hops with concerts, a weekly farmers' market, and other festivities, while in the winter the pond becomes a skating rink, especially popular with office workers in their lunch hour. A Henry Moore sculpture, *The Archer*, was a controversial addition to the square in its early years, because it was so expensive.

Now cross Queen Street towards the Toronto Dominion Bank and continue south down Bay Street. There's a wonderful set of art deco bronze doors at 357 Bay Street, and another magnificent doorway at No 320.

Guarding the vaults

As this has been the financial heart of the city for many years, most of the buildings are owned by financial institutions who tended to compete with each other to see who could produce the most outstanding building. This becomes particularly apparent at the corner of King and Bay streets.

First Canadian Place, to your right, is Toronto's tallest building. Designed by Edward Stone, it has a stunning interior of Italian carrara marble halls and striking murals. On the other side of Bay Street is the old **Bank of Nova Scotia** building, another fine example of art deco, while adjacent to it on King Street, the new and lofty **Scotiabank Plaza** has an elegant interior of Italian red granite. The original Banking Hall of the former **Bank of Commerce** (now Canadian Imperial Bank of Commerce) on the southeast corner, opposite Scotiabank Plaza, is worth a look. The **Toronto Dominion Centre** on the south-west corner was Toronto's first skyscraper, built in the 1960s. The black block has a rather utilitarian appearance but when it was built it was considered a decidedly revolutionary design. Further down Bay Street you come to the old **Toronto Stock Exchange**, another splendid example of art deco now cleverly incorporated into the Ernst & Young Tower. In 1994 the historic trading floor was converted into the **Design Exchange** (234 Bay Street; tel: 416-363-6121; Mon–Fri 10am–6pm, Sat–Sun noon–5pm; www.dx.org), which showcases the work of Canadian designers in fields ranging from architecture and urban design to theatre design and interactive media.

At Wellington Street you'll find **Royal Bank Plaza**, with its 14,000 windows tinted with real gold (always a magnificent sight at sunset).

Turn left and walk east to Yonge Street. Cross the road, turn right and walk down Yonge Street to Front Street, and turn left. On the south side is the **Hummingbird Centre**, formerly the home of the National Ballet of Canada and the Canadian Opera Company, which moved to the Four Seasons Arts Centre in 2006. Internationally renowned architect, Daniel Libeskind, has been commissioned to transform the Hummingbird into an arts centre to showcase work from Toronto's multicultural communities. The next block houses the **St Lawrence Centre for the Arts**, home of the Canadian Stage Company, which produces some of the city's best dramatic productions.

Just past Scott Street, you come to **Berczy Park**. Immediately

Snatching a nap

Flatiron Building

opposite on the south side is a row of Victorian buildings occupied by a number of interesting shops. **Timbuctoo** (No 39) has crafts from all over the world, while literary types will enjoy **Nicholas Hoare** (No 45). With books floor-to-ceiling and comfortable chairs arranged around the fireplace, it's difficult to resist. **Europe Bound** (No 47), whose friendly, knowledgeable staff have, more often than not, 'walked the walk', sells excellent equipment, clothing and shoes for the great outdoors.

There are a number of pubs and restaurants in the next couple of blocks, and **Flatiron's** offers an assortment of Christmas decorations and gifts. On the north side of the road is one of Toronto's most

St Lawrence Market

photographed buildings, the ever-popular **Flatiron Building**. A triangular shaped brick construction, its west exterior wall, which overlooks Berczy Park, features an intriguing mural (which windows are real?) by artist Derek Besant. At 71 Front Street East, look to your left for one of my favourite views – St James's Cathedral framed by Market Square. When it was built in the early 1850s, its 99-m (324 ft) high spire was the tallest in North America, and was a landmark for ships on Lake Ontario.

Now you're in the heart of an area much loved by Torontonians. There's been a market at the intersection of Front and Jarvis streets since 1803, and the **St Lawrence Market** (Tues–Thur 8am–6pm, Fri 8am–7pm, Sat 5am–5pm) is still a big draw.

On Saturday, local farmers, including some traditionally dressed Mennonites, bring their goods to the **North Market** (open from 5am) on the north side of Front Street. On both sides of the street, the aisles are packed, as people jostle, eyeing the best cuts of meat and assessing the fresh fish, vegetables, fruit, cheeses, bagels, and much more. The cries of street vendors often mingle with the hauntingly beautiful melodies of South American musicians busking outside.

Toronto's first City Hall was originally housed in the south side market building. Upstairs in the **Market Gallery** (Wed–Fri 10am–4pm, Sat 9am–4pm, Sun noon–4pm) there's a permanent (and free) exhibition on Toronto's history, and a superb view over the market. If a picnic lunch appeals, buy your victuals here, as you'll soon reach a pleasant city park soon.

Walk north up Jarvis to King Street. East on King is **Arts on King** (169 King Street East), a huge gallery in a restored building where an eclectic selection of Canadian art and craft is on display. The corner building on the southwest corner is the graciously restored **St Lawrence Hall**, Toronto's second city hall. Over the years it has hosted hundreds of gala concerts and banquets, and illustrious celebrities, from opera singer Jenny Lind to P T Barnum's Tom Thumb, have entertained here.

Now head back towards Yonge Street. On the north side of King you come to **St James's Park**, its vibrant flower beds modelled on a 19th-century park, and an agreeable picnic spot to watch the world go by. Beside it is **St James's Cathedral**, a fine example of 19th-century, English Gothic architecture, where there is often a noontime concert.

On the other side of King Street is the **Toronto Sculpture Garden**. You will always find something intriguing to ponder over. You can also enjoy it over lunch at **La Maquette**, a neighbouring eatery with an outdoor patio that is virtually part of the Garden. Or continue along King Street to the regal **King Edward Hotel**, much favoured by visiting dignitaries, for a pleasant lunch in **Café Victoria**.

From the King subway station (at the corner of Yonge), take the train south to Union Station and switch to the LRT street car which links up below ground with the subway line, for a ride down to Harbourfront.

Irrigation in St James's Park

Now you've arrived at one of Toronto's favourite playgrounds. The **Harbourfront Centre** (www.harbourfrontcentre.com) is open year round and puts on an amazingly varied and esoteric programme, catering for many tastes. When you get off the street car, **Pier 6 Centre** is to your left. It's the oldest surviving building (1907) on Toronto's waterfront, and is typical of the port's freight sheds at the end of the 19th century. Now it houses a small café with a patio overlooking the water. Tickets for harbour cruises are sold at a nearby kiosk.

The Harbourfront Centre can occupy the rest of your day and night. There are three main buildings to check out in this waterside park, besides any outdoors activities that may be taking place. The first building, beside the street car stop, is

Tours and T-shirts

Queen's Quay Terminal (daily 10am–6pm), a former warehouse converted into a speciality shop niche – clothing, Inuit sculpture, jewellery, children's toys and restaurants (four beside the water). It's the sort of place where you may end up buying an aerobic frisbee for long distance throwing, or perhaps a metal-and-wire sculpture of a motorcycle. Then there's the **Premier Dance Theatre**, where everything from classical to avant-garde dance is performed by Canadian and international dance companies.

At Dockside, around Queen's Quay, harbour cruise ships line up, with grandiose names such as *Mariposa Belle* or *Empress of Canada*. Harbourfront plays host to all kinds of ships from tall ships to naval vessels.

The next building to the west is the **Power Plant** (Tues–Sun noon–6pm, Wed noon–8pm), a former ice-making factory transformed into a gallery for contemporary art, and the **Harbourfront Centre Theatre**.

Beyond the Power Plant, the **York Quay Centre** is always a hive of activity. Walk towards the street end of the building and go in through the first set of double doors. On your left is the **Harbour-front Craft Studio** (Feb–Dec Tues and Sun 10am–6pm, Wed–Sat 10am–8pm) where self-employed craftspeople make beautiful objects in ceramics, glass, textiles and metal. Boards explaining the various processes hang over the work areas. A small crowd usually gathers by the sweating glass-makers at the fiery furnace. To your right, **Bounty**

Fishy art

33

Harbour traffic

Contemporary Canadian Craft Shop (Tues 11am–6pm, Wed–Fri 11am–8pm, Sat, Sun and holidays 11am–6pm) sells the artists' work.

Go through the second set of doors to a central lobby where there's an information desk. Do check what's going on as you could easily miss something you'd really like to see. Behind the desk is the **Brigantine Room** (tel: 416-973-4760), where the Harbourfront Reading Series takes place weekly all year round. Authors from Canada and across the world come here to read from their latest works and to take part in literary forums and seminars.

Follow the walkway past the Studio Theatre and the York Quay Gallery (more modern art) to the **Photo Passage**, where thought-provoking work by contemporary photographic artists frequently adorns the curving walls. At the end of York Quay is **Lakeside Eats**, and the city's favourite outdoor skating rink.

A drawbridge over the marina takes you to **Pier 4**. The theme here is nautical in the various bars and restaurants and it is also the base for several sailing clubs.

If you're not tired out, the delightful **Toronto Music Garden** (open year-round) is a five-minute walk away, at the southwest corner of Lower Spadina. Designed by the renowned cellist Yo Yo Ma and

Watering hole

landscape designer Julie Moir Messervy, this unique park is a reflection in landscape of Bach's *First Suite for Unaccompanied Cello*. During the summer there are concerts, along with guided or self-guided tours organised by the Harbourfront Centre.

Backtrack to the harbour for a drink or supper by the waterside. **Pearl Harbourfront Chinese Cuisine** has Cantonese and Szechuan specialities and stunning views, while the **Boathouse Bar and Grill** delights the 'wave-watching' crowd.

University and Museums

Breakfast on Bloor Street West in the southern Annex; explore the neighbourhood around the University of Toronto; lunch and the remainder of the day at Royal Ontario Museum and the George R Gardiner Museum of Ceramic Art or the Bata Shoe Museum.

–To the start: take the TTC to Bathurst Street station.–

Bloor Street West, between Spadina Avenue and Bathurst Street, separates the trendy residential area to the north, known as the Annex, from the more colourful, immigrant-based area to the south, inhabited over the years by waves of Jewish, Chinese, Italian and Portuguese newcomers. Consequently, exotic delicatessens mingle with cheap eateries, all offering an enticing variety of ethnic cuisines. Tree-lined streets to the north and south of Bloor Street hint correctly at civilized downtown living.

From Bathurst Street Station turn left towards Bloor Street. Turn left at the corner of Bloor and Bathurst, and there is **Honest Ed's** *(see Shopping, pages 66–68)*. Its flashing orange and yellow sign is impossible to miss! The next few blocks reflect the origins and interests of the local residents, including the **Bloor Cinema** (one of the city's beloved festival cinemas, which feature a superb range of movie classics, as well as more recent productions); **Paupers**, a pub housed in a former bank, which has a great rooftop patio; and **Lee's Palace**, a popular venue for visiting rock bands. A little further along, you'll come to the **Kensington Natural Bakery and Café** (No 460), a potential breakfast spot, and **The Cheese Dairy**, which has a wide-ranging, loyal clientele.

At the corner of Bloor and Borden, **Dooney's Café** is a well established Toronto institution where many of the literary crowd, university professors and neighbourhood characters congregate in a sunny down-to-earth setting. Their loyal customers include a group of Hungarian Jewish holocaust survivors, who have come every weekday afternoon for years – some from the far northern reaches of the city. It opens at 10am, so if you've already breakfasted, at least stop by for coffee (their cappuccino is highly recommended) and enjoy the friendly service.

From here, continue east on Bloor, where you will find esoteric books at **Seekers**

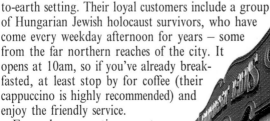

Honest Ed's

Downtown doorway

Books (No 509), exquisite jewellery at **Inti Crafts** (No 444) and intriguing gifts at **Eternal Moment** (No 497). Head right down Brunswick, passing the **Poor Alex Theatre**, one of Toronto's alternative theatres, then go left on Sussex and right on Major. Within five minutes you'll reach Harbord Street, having passed a typical mix of downtown homes, some with stained-glass windows, shiny brass door knockers and colourful flower boxes, others that are somewhat less immaculate.

Turn left on Harbord. You'll see **Harbord Bakery** (No 115) across the street, where Saturday morning visits are *de rigeur* for Annex residents. A little further east on the north side, **Momo's** (No 116) is a popular Middle Eastern café. In the two blocks between Major Street and Spadina Avenue there are five excellent bookstores, including two antiquarian booksellers, **East West Books** (No 128) and **Atticus Books** (No 84). The **Caversham Bookseller** (No 98) specialises in books on counselling, and the **Women's Book Store** (No 73) speaks for itself. **Wonder Works** (No 79A) has alternative books and gifts of a holistic nature. One of Toronto's most famous restaurants, **Splendido** *(see Eating Out, pages 69–72)* is adjacent to Atticus Books.

Cross Spadina Avenue, and you are now entering the domain of the **University of Toronto**. At the northeast corner of Spadina is the University's Graduate House, with its dramatic cantilevered cornice – ending in a giant O – hanging over Harbord Street, marking the western gateway to the St George campus.

The large complex to your right is the Athletics Centre. At St George Street, Harbord jigs to the left, and continues as Hoskin Avenue. The rather curious building at the corner of Harbord and St George is the **John P Robarts Research Library**, which is occasionally referred to as Fort Book. The rather fine, turreted building on the northeast corner of Hoskin and St George is the Catholic-based **Newman Centre**.

This is your opportunity to explore the University campus, with its tree-lined walkways, stately courtyards and elegant buildings. There are also free guided walking tours in the summer (tel: 416-978-5000; Mon–Fri 11am and 2pm, Sat and Sun 11am), which leave from Hart House. Turn down Tower Road at the eastern end of the playing fields, so named for **The Soldiers' Tower** ahead of you, a memorial to the men and women who lost their lives in active service during World Wars I and II.

Imposing campus sculpture

Queen's Park

Beyond the archway, **Hart House** is the late-Gothic, Oxbridge-styled limestone building to your left. The social centre for the university, its **Great Hall** has hosted many famous world leaders. A quote from John Milton on freedom of expression circles the walls. Classical concerts are often held here, while jazz sessions frequently take place in the quadrangle and common rooms. Exhibitions of some outstanding Canadian art are held in rotation in the **Justina M Barnicke Art Gallery** (tel: 416-978-8398 for details).

In front of Hart House, the **Stewart Observatory** is the oldest building on campus, built in 1814, although it was moved to its current site in 1905.

Depending on your time and inclination, wander along King's College Circle. West of Hart House is **University College**, a neo-Romanesque building housing the first chemistry laboratory in Canada, **Croft Chapter House**. It was known as the 'godless college' after its establishment as a university free from social exclusiveness and religious control in 1853. Next on the Circle is **Knox College**, the Presbyterian theology school, much loved by film and video makers because of its impressive gardens and Gothic architecture.

Backtrack to Hoskin Avenue, cross the road, turn right and go past Trinity College to **Queen's Park**. The park was named after Queen Victoria in 1860, and is still a peaceful haven in the heart of Toronto. It's a favourite haunt of harried civil servants from the nearby Ontario

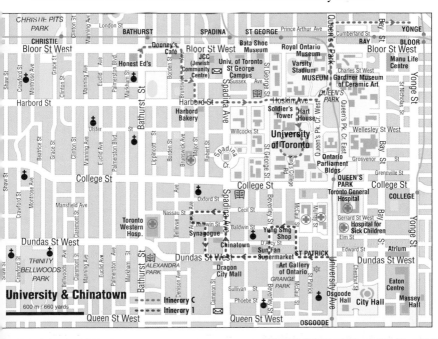

University & Chinatown

600 m / 660 yards

- - - - Itinerary C
- - - - Itinerary 1

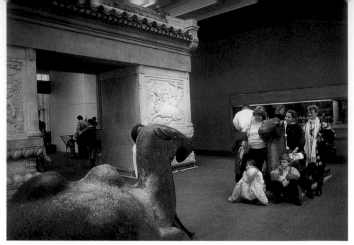

Chinese exhibits at the ROM

Legislature buildings, and of thousands of University of Toronto students. Turn left and walk north. Within minutes, you will have arrived at the **Royal Ontario Museum** (100 Queen's Park; tel: 416-586-8000; Sun–Thur 10am–6pm, Fri 10am–9.30pm). If you are feeling hungry, there are many restaurants in the vicinity. The museum (known locally as ROM) is undergoing a major expansion, which, when complete will have three restaurants including the Rotunda Café. On part of the complex is the luminous **Michael Lee-Chin Crystal** building – designed by architect, Daniel Libeskind – that will house six additional galleries. Some of the original galleries are also being renovated. However, the museum remains open throughout the construction and is still well worth visiting.

The ROM is the only museum in North America to house art, archaeology and science under one roof. Tours (no charge) are offered during the day starting at 11am with a general tour; the rest focus on specific galleries.

The galleries on the first floor house the ROM's Asian collection, which is world-renowned – its Chinese collection is one of the finest outside China. The **Bishop White Gallery** is a stunning collection of Chinese temple art, with three huge wall paintings (painted around AD1300) and 14 massive wooden Buddhist sculptures created between the 12th and 15th centuries. Even if you know nothing about ancient Chinese temple art, the gallery is awe-inspiring. **T. T. Tsui Galleries of Chinese Art** span more than 6,000 years of Chinese history, and an actual Chinese tomb complex of huge 14th-to 17th-century stone sculptures can be seen in the **Matthews Family Chinese Sculpture Court** and the **Gallery of Chinese Architecture**. The **Prince Takamado Gallery of Japan** has been created to house the ROM's Japanese art, which is the largest collection in Canada.

The second floor is devoted to the Natural Sciences. One of the most popular galleries – for children at least – is the **Bat Cave**, a replica of parts of the 3-km (2-mile) long St Clair Cave in Jamaica. An eerie tour is followed by an exhibition on the 900 known species of bats. The CIBC **Discovery Room** is also popular with the museum's younger visitors. Here they can try on armour, touch a 1.5 billion-

Dinosaur Gallery

year-old fossil or write their name in hieroglyphs in this interactive 'mini-museum'.

The technological, historical, artistic and social development of ancient civilizations are the focus of the third floor. In the **Greek World** there's a spectacular sculpture court featuring 20 classical sculptures from the 4th century BC to the 1st century AD. Other galleries highlight Early Italy and the Etruscans, Bronze- and Iron-Age Europe, Imperial Rome, Byzantium, Islam, the Ancient Egypt Gallery, and the Nubia Gallery. During term time, you may have to weave your way around school groups, especially in the Ancient Egypt Gallery, but it's worth it. The achievements of these ancient civilizations are astonishing. A personal favourite is the Islam gallery, set up as an Islamic city, in which you can visit a mosque, a shrine, a house, a garden and a market.

Directly opposite the ROM is the **Gardiner Museum of Ceramic Art** (111 Queen's Park, tel: 416-586-8080; daily 10am–6pm; www. gardinermuseum.on.ca). Closed for renovations until Spring 2006, it is a gem, and the expanded space will have over 2,800 pieces spanning some 3,000 years, displayed in 12 galleries. The first floor will have galleries devoted to Ancient American, English, and 15th- and 16th-century Italian majolica and contemporary pottery.

Upstairs at the Gardiner, 18th-century continental and English porcelain and Asian porcelain is on display, including valuable pieces from Augustus II's porcelain factory in Meissen, Germany and a fabulous collection from the Du Paquier collection, Meissen's Viennese rival. *The Monkey Band*, created between 1749 and 1753 by Johann Joachim Kändler at the Meissen factory is enchanting, as are the 18th-century *commedia dell'arte* figurines, including characters such as Pantaloon and Harlequin, produced at both German and English factories.

The nearby **Bata Shoe Museum** (327 Bloor Street West, tel: 416-979-7799; Tues–Wed, Fri–Sat 10am–5pm, Thur 10–8pm, Sun noon–5pm; June–Aug also Mon 10am–5pm; admission charge; www.batashoemuseum.ca) is a delightful alternative to the Gardiner Museum. Its collection of more than 10,000 shoes spans over 4,500 years of footwear, from ancient funerary sandals to Chinese silk shoes, *haute couture* pumps and a display of celebrity's shoes including some of Elton John's outrageous platforms.

Depending upon where you finish up – when you have absorbed as much as you can – the Museum subway station is at the ROM's main entrance, or the St George subway is across the road from the Bata Shoe Museum.

Gardiner Museum ceramic

Option 1. Chinatown and Kensington Market

Two of Toronto's most vibrant neighbourhoods reside on each other's doorsteps. Together they add up to a full morning of people, food and non-stop hustle. As the tour ends two blocks from the Art Gallery of Ontario, it could be combined with Option 6 to make a full day. For itinerary route see map on page 37.

–To the start: TTC to St Patrick subway station.–

The Chinese are one of Toronto's fastest-growing ethnic groups, and their 259,000-strong community is spread over five Chinatowns. However, this walking tour focuses on the main downtown **Chinatown** – always intriguing, ever frenetic, every day of the week.

From the St Patrick station, start at Gerling Global House on the northwest corner of University Avenue and Dundas Street West, and walk west on the north side of Dundas. At McCaul Street, the street signs become bilingual, in Mandarin and English. Turn right on McCaul, go two blocks to Baldwin Street, then turn left.

This part of Baldwin is a blend of old and new. Besides several popular, European-style restaurants and cafés, there's the **Yung Sing Pastry Shop** (No 22), one of the oldest Chinese pastry shops in Toronto, famous for its tofu and barbecued meat buns, and **Wah Sing Seafood Restaurant** (No 47), highly rated for its bargain-value lobster and crab, served with a potent ginger or black bean sauce.

Turn left on Beverley Street, then right on Dundas Street. Every other business appears to be a restaurant, and the street is packed with bustling shoppers. Fruit and vegetable stalls overflow with all kinds of exotica, while in grocery stores such as **Yong Xing Supermarket** (No 435) the shelves are brimming with endless varieties of soy sauce, snack packets of dried squid and cuttlefish, dried bamboo and lotus leaves. At **Ten Ren's Tea House** (No 454) you might catch a demonstration of the ancient tea ceremony. They sell over 120 varieties of tea – black, green, oolong (a combination of the first two), twig and herbal – priced from $20 to $160 for 450g (about 1lb).

Shopping in Chinatown

If you're ready for a break, visit the **Tachong Restaurant and Bakery** (No 492). Moon cakes are one of their specialities, made from white lotus paste, but they also offer a wide variety of rolls, croissants and tarts. It's a favourite stop for local shoppers.

At Spadina Avenue turn right. The pavements are invariably crowded, since there are bargains to be had whether you're looking for food, clothing or leather goods. On the southwest corner of Dundas and Spadina, **Dragon City** is a soaring, brightly lit mall covered with Chinese script. Inside is a wide range of products sold throughout two jam-packed floors by independent businesses such as **My Heart Lingerie, Dai Kuang Wah Herbs, Wing Hing Ginseng and Health Products** and **Wing Cheung Jewellery**. You'll also find a multitude of stores selling custom-made shoes and boots, inexpensive electronics and imported clothing.

Cross the road and continue north up Spadina. **King's Noodle House** (No 296) makes its own noodles on the premises, and is renowned for its various barbecued dishes. Wending your way through the crowds, you'll pass emporia such as the **Tap Phong Trading Company** (No 360), where you can browse amongst woks, and huge ceramic pots, delicate Chinese screens and much more. At Nassau Street, take a left turn.

You are now approaching **Kensington Market**. The market began when Jewish immigrants from central and southern Europe moved here in the 1920s and 1930s. They were largely supplanted in the 1950s by Portuguese incomers, who have since been joined by the Chinese and Caribbean communities.

A Portuguese radio station is at one corner of Nassau and Augusta Avenue, while two fruit markets, operated by families of long-standing in the area, occupy two other corners. Turn left on Augusta and you come to shops selling everything from padlocks and buttons to hats, dresses, used clothing and leather goods. **Harry David Ltd** (No 220) has been selling men's dress and work wear at bargain prices for more than 50 years. **Amadeu's** (No 184), a short block south of Baldwin Street, is a cheap Portuguese seafood restaurant with adjoining bar.

Much of the joy of visiting Kensington Market is gained from the people you see and the snippets of conversation

Chestnuts for sale

Cheerful stall holder

you catch. Noisy but cheerful haggling – often in Portuguese – over live chickens and rabbits is more likely to be heard on Baldwin Street, one block south, on which you must turn left. For a healthy, tasty snack, **Mexican Food** (No 200) offers roasted cashews and sun-dried fruit. Across the street, **New Seaway Fish Market** announces specials such as live carp. In **Chocolate Addict** (No 185), you'll spot more than 20 flavours of truffles, handmade from the finest Belgian chocolate, and a sign claiming that if you have melted chocolate on your hands, you're eating it too slowly. **Patty King** (No 187) is an old-time Caribbean bakeshop where you can taste homemade mango smoothies, spicy patties and Jamaican-style beef. **European Meat Market** (No 176) offers the 'best deals in town', while enticing smells waft out from **My Market Bakery** (No 172), which sells Portuguese buns and Montréal-style bagels.

Turn right on Kensington Avenue. On your right, the **Global Cheese Shoppe** and **Mendel's Creamery** will tempt cheese lovers, and if you're getting peckish, the **Kensington Café** (No 73) offers inexpensive soups, pasta and sandwiches.

Of interest is the **Anshei Minsk Synagogue** (10 St Andrews, tel: 416-595-5723) down a small street to the left, one block south of Baldwin Street. Built in 1930 in a combination Russian and Romanesque style, it welcomes visitors to its daily services.

Back on Kensington, continue south. Closer to Dundas Street, you may feel as though you've stepped back into the 1960s. You'll find vintage Levis at one shop, oil and incense at another, and second-hand clothing shops such as **Last Temptation** and **Courage My Love**.

At Dundas, turn left and walk back towards University. Restaurants, shops, herbalists and established Canadian financial institutions with their names in Mandarin all vie for your attention. Again, the unusual smells and sights are almost overwhelming, but it's impossible not to feel energized by the bustle and noise of the largest immigrant group in Toronto. Cantonese is the second most common language spoken here and as you continue east, you'll pass the offices of *Sing Tao Daily* (No 417), the largest of the three daily Chinese newspapers.

Global Cheese Shoppe

Option 2. The Beaches

Much beloved by Torontonians, especially at weekends, The Beaches is a California-style, laid-back neighbourhood known for its Boardwalk, a 20-block promenade beside Lake Ontario; its New England clapboard-and-shingle homes; and Queen Street East, with its eclectic mix of boutiques, book shops, antiques shops and cafés.

–To the start: take the No 501 street car east along Queen Street to Wood-bine Avenue.–

All you need for a visit to **The Beaches** is time, and comfortable walking shoes. Should you even consider coming out by car, be warned that parking is practically impossible, particularly at weekends. Years ago, The Beaches used to be 'cottage country' for Torontonians eager to escape the hurly burly of city life. Now it's barely a 30-minute ride from downtown. Don't be put off by the dreary approach. It will soon become clear why The Beaches is one of the most desirable Toronto neighbourhoods in which to live. Somehow, particularly in the warm summer months, it still feels like a small resort, far from the city.

The Beaches Boardwalk

An Englishman named Joseph Williams was one of the first settlers in the area, in the early 1850s. By 1879 he had created his own pleasure park, **Kew Gardens**, based on its English namesake. Soon, cottages sprang up among the trees, and canoe clubs dotted the waterfront. However, it wasn't until the extension of the street car tracks along Queen Street in the late 19th century that 'downtowners' began to descend on The Beaches in droves, to picnic and to dance the summer nights away. Gradually, as the city grew, and transport improved, the area became a year-round residential area.

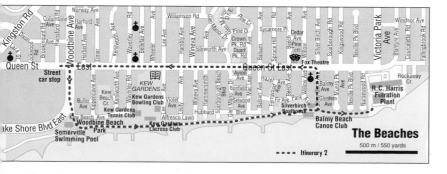

Get off the street car at Woodbine Avenue and walk south, towards the lake. Go past the **Somerville Swimming Pool** (free admission to its three pools, including one that's Olympic size) to join the **Boardwalk**. As you turn east, Lake Ontario and a wide stretch of sandy beach are on your right, and **Woodbine Beach Park** is to your left. Large, weathered maples stand guard between the Boardwalk and **Trillium Trail**, a narrow biking and jogging path – stray on to this at your peril, especially at weekends, when the Boardwalk and the cycling path are crowded. Dogs on long leashes and small children (unleashed) revel in the freedom of the beach and parkland. On a fine day, seagulls and Canada geese soar overhead, while sailboats and wind-surfers skim across the waves in a seemingly effortless manner.

Soon you will come to a cluster of community clubs, the **Kew Gardens Tennis Club**, the **Kew Gardens Lacrosse Club**, and the **Kew Gardens Bowling Greens**. There are plenty of benches if you feel like watching for a while. If you cut across to Lee Avenue on the eastern side of Kew Gardens, you will see there's only one house on the west side of the street, No 30. It was built by Kew Williams, son of Joseph (and, yes, named after his father's favourite gardens), as a wedding present for his bride in the early 1900s.

Walk east along Alfresco Lawn to Wineva Avenue and rejoin the Boardwalk. For a few blocks, the roads extend to meet it. On either side, ancient trees proffer shade to the New England-style houses clapboards and the more formal, Edwardian-style brick dwellings. Many of the street names – such as Hazel, Silverbirch, Pine, Willow, Bracken and Balsam – reflect the area's arboreal origins.

Continue along the Boardwalk, past the **Balmy Beach Canoe Club**. At Silverbirch Avenue, you'll come to the **Silverbirch Boathouse**, where you can borrow volleyball equipment, or bucket and spades for children, at no cost. If you're not ready to leave the water, continue along the sandy beach. Enticing gardens back onto the beach here, and eventually you will arrive at the **R C Harris Filtration Plant**. Built in the 1930s, it's a striking art deco edifice that has been compared to a Mayan temple. Rising over the

Ready for action

Leafy suburbs

lake on a vast, grassy slope, it's an intriguing diversion.

Backtrack to Silverbirch and walk up to Queen Street East. At No 70, the Healthy Earth Bilingual Nursery School reflects the political correctness of many Beaches residents. Cross to the north side of Queen Street and turn left. Notice the lovely old apartment buildings at Willow and Queen. Fortunately, the blight of high-rise buildings has not penetrated The Beaches.

Now is the time for some serious browsing. Coffee lovers will enjoy **Remarkable Bean** (No 2242) with its limited edition coffees and chessboard tables. As you continue west, you will see across the street the **Fox Theatre**. For decades, a visit to this movie review theatre followed by a Chinese meal at the **Garden Gate** opposite, has been a popular, inexpensive evening out for Torontonians. Study the unusual mural outside **Quigley's** (No 2232), known for its Sunday jazz sessions (4–7pm), and then check out **Nature's Joy** (No 2230), a shop specialising in holistic skincare, incense and tranquillity fountains. On the other side of the street, at **Art2 Jewellery** (No 2359), you'll find jewellery (including a selection designed by owner Gill Birol), ceramics, handbags and shawls, all handcrafted by Canadian artisans.

At **Beadworks** (No 2154) there's a dazzling collection of crystal, Indian glass, Venetian and hand-painted wooden beads, offering great potential for creating your own accessories. You can even sign up for a workshop.

By now, chances are you're ready for refreshment. **La Tea Da** (No 2305) is a bright, cheery tearoom with delicious freshly baked scones served with traditional high, afternoon and cream teas. Another option is **Pam Coffee and Tea Company** (No 2142), which offers a vast selection of coffees, teas, ice creams and pastries in a cosy, welcoming setting. Or you could opt for sushi and noodles at **Japango** (No 2209), or the mouth-watering line-up of hand-crafted Belgian chocolates and homemade fudge at the **Nutty Chocolatier** (No 2179). Perhaps join the locals at the **Sunset Grill** (No 2006) for burgers and all-day breakfasts.

There's also **Lick's Homeburgers & Ice Cream** (No 1960), a non-typical selection of pub-style food at **Lion on the Beach** (No 1958), and an international mix of Malaysian, Québec and Cajun fare amidst old Canadiana surroundings at **Whitlock's** (No 1961).

You can spend endless hours at The Beaches, morning, noon and night. Throughout the summer there's a full programme of activities, from Beach fests and children's festivals, to jazz concerts, art exhibitions and walking tours. When you've exhausted your energy, return downtown on the westbound Queen street car.

A tour of Rogers Centre, the renamed SkyDome, the world's first multi-purpose stadium with a retractable roof, followed by lunch in the Hard Rock Café or Club Windows.

—To the start: TTC to Union Station, then follow directional signs to the indoor pedestrian walkway that connects Union Station to Rogers Centre.—

One-hour tours of the magnificent **Rogers Centre** (tel: 416-341-2770; www.rogerscentre.com) are offered daily, depending on the event schedule. You don't have to be interested in sports to enjoy the novelty and magnitude of this mega-project.

At the northeast corner of Rogers Centre, take a moment to savour *The Audience*, 14 large, cartoon-like figures sculpted by Michael Snow. Then purchase your ticket for the tour.

The ballpark has been home to the Toronto Blue Jays baseball team and the Toronto Argonauts Canadian football team since 1989. During the early construction stages, in 1986, a team of archaeologists remained on site to examine and rescue valuable finds. As a result, at the beginning of your tour, you pass through an exhibition mounted by the Toronto Historic Board of some of the 1,400 artefacts that were uncovered during the excavation. Besides an assortment of bottles, chinaware and glassware used by Torontonians in the 1800s, significant findings include the remains of **Navy Wharf** (dating back to 1817) and a French cannon built between 1725 and 1750 that was probably used during the War of 1812.

The tour continues with a 15-minute film, *The Inside Story*, which focuses on an illuminating brain-storming session between Roderick Robbie, the architect, and Michael Allen, the engineer, as they tussled with the SkyDome concept. At times their exuberant exchanges seem more philosophical than practical in nature. The actual and awesome mechanics of building the roof, while battling with the elements, are also vividly described by one of the team of construction workers who banged in 250,000 bolts using 2.7-kg (6-lb) sledgehammers.

The stadium took 2½ years to build, and opened with a Blue Jays game on 5 June, 1989. You'll be inundated with facts and trivia as you walk through the various levels, visiting the press box and a private luxury suite along the way. The five levels of seating accommodate 52,000 for baseball games, 53,000 for football matches, and from 10,000 to 60,000 for concerts and other special events. Covering 3.2 hectares (8 acres), the roof consists of four panels, three of which retract. It glides to an open or shut position at a rate of 21m (71ft) per minute in just 20 minutes. The steel parabolic arches span more

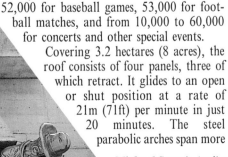

Michael Snow's Audience

Blue Jays at the Rogers Centre

than 205m (674ft) at the widest point, and are strong enough to bear up to 4.5-m (15-ft) snow drifts.

A state-of-the-art, integrated scoring and display system includes a 33.5-m long by 10.6-m-wide (110ft by 35ft) video screen, with more than 604,000 pixels, which replaces the old JumboTron. On either side of the main screen, two monochrome LED video displays – each 3m (10ft) high and 18m (59ft) wide   show the pitch count, speed and type. Most dramatic of all, perhaps, are the two ribbon boards that encircle most of the 300 level. Measuring 1.2 m (4ft) high and 132.6m (435ft) long, they are used for 'in-game entertaining' – to excite the crowds during the game.

To date, the stadium's largest crowd – almost 70,000 strong – came to see Hulk Hogan in Wrestlemania. However, 58,000 came to see the band Genesis, 50,000 filed through the gates to watch the final game when the Blue Jays won the 1992 World Series, and 36,000 turned up to watch the final episode of *Cheers*.

At some point along the tour, you'll get to sit and gaze out over the recently installed deep green turf, that is said to be virtually indistinguishable from grass. Known as FieldTurf, it apparently plays exactly like natural grass. Made from long fibres of polyethylene that are anchored in a mix of cryogenic rubber and silica sand, the rubber-and-sand combination provides a similar experience to the give and take of natural grass, so players don't have to worry about burns when they dive for the ball. Despite the vastness, Rogers Centre is not intimidating. For all the awesome technology, it's the people on the field and in the stands who create its magical moments.

After so much excitement – and so many statistics – you'll be ready for lunch. Try the **Hard Rock Café** (beside Gate 1, tel: 416-341-2388) for an inexpensive lunch surrounded by rock 'n' roll memorabilia, or **Club Windows** (tel: 416-341-2424) with its 50 monitors to provide play-by-play action commentary if you're eating there during a game.

Ontario Science Centre appeals to all age groups, and a passion for science is not a prerequisite for an afternoon of enjoyment.

–To the start: easily reached by TTC. Either take Yonge Street subway north to Eglinton station, transfer to the Eglinton East bus and get off at Don Mills Road, or take the Bloor Street subway east to Pape and transfer to the Don Mills bus, which stops in front of the Science Centre (770 Don Mills Road). There is plentiful parking if you decide to drive.–

One of the initial goals of the **Ontario Science Centre** (tel: 416-696-1000; daily 10am–5pm; www.OntarioScienceCentre.ca), back in 1969, was that it be a place of fun, and should arouse curiosity. While the fun certainly remains, the centre is being transformed into a place where the emphasis is on 'personal innovation'. Today visitors – and particularly young people – are being challenged to come up with ideas to address real world problems. If that sounds intimidating, don't worry – it's wonderfully designed and user-friendly!

Exhibit hall at Science Centre

The centre's three buildings are perched on a steep hillside that plunges down to the **Don River Valley** 27m (90ft) below. They are connected by glassed-in escalators, with glorious views overlooking the wooded ravine. Beside the main entrance is the **Omnimax Theatre**, a powerful motion-picture system that takes you diving into the deepest ocean or soaring through space. Admission ($) is not included in the basic entrance fee.

In the **Great Hall**, which sits atop the valley, setting-sensitive artworks based on the themes of earth, air, fire and water provide an inspirational place to relax at either end of your visit. From here, follow the signs and descend to Level C.

Immediately to your left as you reach Level C is **Exploring Space**. (You should probably arrange when and where to meet up with your companions, as it's easy to be diverted.) Among the many options here, you can experience blast-off, a lunar landing and the first steps on the moon through the eyes of an Apollo astronaut. In the area beside the **Star Lab Planetarium**, you can learn about eclipses, the moon, tides and orbits.

At the entrance to **KidSpark**, a large sign declares, 'Adults must be accompanied by children'. This learn-through-play space is pure heaven for kids of eight and under. They can discover how water behaves when it flows; build a skeleton or take it apart; and in the music area, they can perform in a real studio, match sounds and make amazing music with a variety of instruments.

When you can tear the children away, proceed down to Level D, where some of the biggest changes are taking place. In the **Weston Family Innovation Centre** you can explore what's hot in science and technology. The vast, multimedia **Hot Zone** amounts to a 'scientific Times Square'. The regularly changing content explores current news, poses topical questions, seeks opinions (would you wear a microchip identifier? Are humans an endangered species?), sparks debate and highlights recent discoveries. And you'll read first-person reports from scientists around the world – perhaps investigating climate change in the Arctic or working on health projects in Cambodia. In the **Challenge Zone**, a different real-world challenge is set daily – such as how can a drought-stricken Brazilian village carry water to its crops without the use of electrical power or manual labour?

Still on Level D, **The Living Earth** explores earth's ever changing ecosystems. There's even a rain forest, complete with a computer-controlled year-round climate of 28°C (82°F) and almost 100 percent humidity. Four different species of endangered poison-dart frogs – safely ensconced in their own climate-controlled homes – live here, as do stick insects and leaf cutter ants. Throughout the exhibit, the global effects of the destruction of the world's rain forests are all too clearly spelt out.

A walk in the rain forest

The inner-workings of your own mind, and other people's, are the focus of **Communications**, where you can delve into the complex workings of the living brain, or test your memory by witnessing a crime and then attempting to identify the criminal. You will also find out how easy it is to be duped through auditory illusions and differentiating sounds.

A fascinating, stand-alone exhibition here is **A Question of Truth**, which examines bias, racism and sexism, and how they've affected scientific practice through history. The highlight of the **Science Arcade** is a show on electricity presented by a cheery young technician who has a way with children (in no time at all they are clamouring to answer questions). The grand finale – selecting someone from the audience with a long mane to have their hair 'electrified' – is a crowd-pleaser every time. At the Ontario Science Centre the old cliché about time passing quickly when you're having fun – even when you're learning too – proves itself once again.

49

A ferry to Centre Island for an afternoon exploring the four main islands – Centre, Ward's, Algonquin and Hanlan's Point – by bicycle, tram or on foot. Weather and time permitting, stay to enjoy a sunset over downtown Toronto.

–To the start: TTC to Union Station, then take the LRT to the ferry terminals at the foot of Bay Street.–

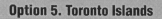

Toronto Islands is a 243-hectare (600-acre) park that, centuries ago, was a long sand bar curving westward from Scarborough Bluffs, east of Toronto. It formed a sheltered bay that Lieutenant Colonel Simcoe deemed ideal for a harbour. Thus, the town of York was founded in the early 1790s.

Island ferry

The **Toronto Islands** ferry service (tel: 416-392-8193) to Ward's Island, Centre Island and Hanlan's Point runs regularly between 6.35am and 11.45pm during the summer. Between Thanksgiving (mid-October) and mid-April, the service is limited, so check the schedule in advance. Two restaurants and several concession stands operate under the auspices of the Parks Department, during summer only, while two cafés on **Ward's Island** are run by local islanders (with somewhat erratic hours). There are also plenty of delightful picnic spots – on beaches, amongst the trees or at the water's edge. (A visit during the winter is an entirely different

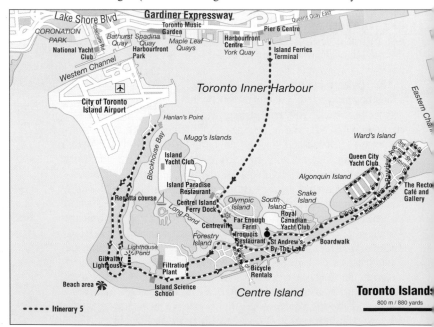

matter, of course. But if you rent a pair of ice skates, there can be some divine skating on some of the islands' lagoons.)

The 10-minute ferry ride to Centre Island is one of the best ways to enjoy Toronto's waterfront, busy with water taxis, yachts, and more commercial traffic. On arrival, follow signs to **Bicycle Rentals**, on the south side of the island. If you prefer walking, the distance from Centre Island Dock to Hanlan's Point is just under 4km (about 2½ miles) and about 2.5km (1½ miles) to Ward's Island. A 'trackless train' also regularly circles between the Centre Island Dock and Hanlan's Point.

Bridge over peaceful waters

Severe storms first separated the peninsula from the mainland in 1828. By the mid-19th century, city residents were flocking to the islands to escape the summer heat. Cottages, hotels, an amusement park, even a baseball stadium all sprang up, particularly at Hanlan's Point. **Centre Island** is the most manicured of the group, with its orderly flower beds, fountains and lagoons, and it is always the most crowded.

At the rental shop, you can choose between ordinary bicycles, tandems and two- or four-seater quadricycles. Turn right as you leave the bike rental shop and set off towards **Ward's Island**. The path hugs the shoreline, and soon you will be riding along the somewhat narrower **Boardwalk**. There's no obvious demarkation between Centre Island and Ward's Island but once you come to folksy little cottages, you will know you have arrived. The **Rectory Café & Gallery** fronts on to the Boardwalk, and may be open.

A cottage community grew up on Ward's and Algonquin islands during the 1920s and 1930s. To this day, the island community is known for its 'alternative' lifestyle, and it has had a long-running battle with city politicians over property ownership. Some islanders are former flower children, but all are committed to island living, year-round. Take time to cycle up and down the narrow streets. Some of the homes have been delightfully spruced up, others, in truth, are somewhat dilapidated. Make your way down to the Ward's Island Ferry Dock, follow the path on the city side, and head back towards Centre Island. Don't be deterred by the steep bridge over to **Algonquin Island** – it's a worthwhile detour. The streets are named after First Nations,

Forever blowing bubbles

a reminder that before the Europeans' arrival, local tribes also regarded the area as a healthy and pleasurable spot to relax.

Return to Ward's and continue your journey, with yacht clubs to your right and parkland to your left. One of Toronto's most prestigious sailing clubs, the **Royal Canadian Yacht Club**, is based here. When the road branches, keep to the right. Soon you will come to **St Andrews-by-the-Lake Church**, built in 1884, the only surviving remnant of the original cottage community.

Go past the bridge to the main Centre Island park, turn right and follow the path beside the water. This stretch is where the Hong Kong Dragon Boat Races take place each summer. Eventually the path curves to the left, and shortly thereafter joins the trail out to **Hanlan's Point**.

On your left, you'll pass the **Island Natural Science School**, where mainland children get a taste of island living. Check out the **Franklin Children's Garden**, inspired by a popular series of books about Franklin the Turtle. This interactive, playful garden includes a Hide & Seek Garden, a pond full of turtles and frogs, a Snail Trail to the Islands' highest point and free storytelling. On the right, beside a stocked trout pond, is **Gibraltar Lighthouse**, built with Queenston limestone in 1806, and Toronto's oldest surviving official building. Detour to the south shore beach for some sunbathing or even swimming (only in August unless you're really hardy) – you'll have it largely to yourself on weekdays. When the road divides, take the left-hand branch, past tennis courts and the periphery of the airport, to the road's end at Hanlan's Point Ferry Dock.

Hanlan's Point is named after a family that settled here in 1862. One son, Ned Hanlan, later became a world-champion rower. By the 1890s, it was a thriving resort, and in 1910 the aforementioned baseball stadium was built, in which Babe Ruth, a baseball legend, hit his first professional home run. During the 1930s, the stadium closed down, the amusement park was demolished, and construction began on **Toronto Island Airport**. Now the take-offs and landings of small aircraft are the main activity at Hanlan's Point. Follow the left-hand road, past graceful willow trees, picnic benches, and yachts with fanciful names tied up at their moorings. Eventually you'll rejoin the main route, and be on the home stretch to return your bike.

Those of you accompanied by children will unquestionably spend some time at **Centreville** and **Far Enough Farm**. Bumper boat rides, log flume rides, pony rides and a

Royal Yacht Club

Toronto's sparkling skyline

giant ferris wheel are the order of the day, and a guaranteed hit with the junior brigade.

If you didn't bring a picnic, substantial refreshments are available at the **Island Paradise Restaurant**, beside the Centre Island Docks, and the **Iroquois Restaurant** closer to Centreville. For a magical end to the day, find a bench on the city side of the islands, and watch the setting sun cast a warm red glow over downtown Toronto as the lights of the city begin to be switched on. Only then will you be ready to catch the ferry back to the city.

Option 6. Art Gallery of Ontario

The Art Gallery of Ontario owns the world's largest collection of Henry Moore sculptures, and an impressive collection of Inuit and contemporary Canadian art, as well as the works of numerous masters.

Moore's Two Forms

–To the start: TTC to St Patrick subway station.–

Follow the directional signs from the subway station and walk west for three short blocks. When you reach Henry Moore's *Two Forms*, at the corner of McCaul Street and Dundas Street West (frequently with one or two youngsters climbing through and around it), you will have arrived at the **Art Gallery of Ontario** (tel: 416-979-6648; Tues, Thur and Fri 11am–6pm, Wed 11am–8.30pm, weekends 11am–5.30pm; no admission charge, or 'pay-what-you can').

In April 2005 the AGO commenced a three-year, $500 million expansion. Upon completion, the Frank Gehry-designed project will increase the art-viewing space by 47 percent – a development largely

triggered by several major donations, including more than 10,000 works of art.

The AGO's already impressive permanent collection, of more than 38,000 works, ranges from 13th-century European paintings to international contemporary works of art and Canadian art, including the Inuit works. One of the largest of the donations is a group of 2,000 works of art from the **Thomson Collection**. Its Canadian art content encompasses works from the 19th to mid-20th century, with a particular emphasis on the paintings of Cornelius Krieghoff and the Group of Seven. Of more than 200 Group of Seven paintings acquired by the AGO, 79 are by the artist Tom Thomson.

The Thomson gift also includes medieval Renaissance and baroque sacred and secular works of art and a decorative arts collection of more than 500 objects – many of international significance, such as the legendary 12th-century Malmesbury Châsse, a selection of baroque ivories, and a group of portrait miniatures dating from 1550 to 1850. Another highlight is Peter Paul Rubens' rediscovered masterpiece, *The Massacre of the Innocents*, which will have its own exhibition space.

The AGO will also feature acquisitions of outstanding collections of historical African and Australian aboriginal art, the Fick-Eggert Archive, which includes more than 300 works on paper, and documents from the circle of early 20th-century artists who make up the avant-garde Cologne Dada group.

Among the landmark additions to the AGO will be a magnificent, glass-enclosed sculpture gallery that will extend 137m (450ft) across the Dundas Street side of the building. On the south side, overlooking Grange Park, a centre for contemporary art will feature 20th-century paintings and sculptures, which is likely to include the works of August Rodin, Amedeo Modigliani, Augustus John, Joan Miró, Marc Chagall and Paul Gauguin, as well as more recently donated masterpieces by Paul-Émile Borduas and Jean-Paul Riopelle.

During the transition, a number of the galleries will be closed. However, beloved favourites from the AGO's collection will continue to be displayed, on rotation, during the construction. For much of that time, a special exhibition entitled **Favourites: Your Choices from our Collection** will be mounted, partly based on information gained from members of the public on the gallery's website, ensuring that the most popular works from its collection can be visited throughout the expansion works. To date, the most votes have gone to Laura Muntz Lyall's *Interesting Story 1898*, a gentle depiction of two children engrossed in a book, Claude Monet's 1879 *Vetheuil in Summertime*, Tom Thomson's *West Wind* and August John's *Marchesa Casati*. There have also been many votes for particular works by the Group of Seven artists and Impressionist landscapes.

As further enticement, the AGO is organising a series of visiting exhibitions, such as *Catherine the Great*, in which more than 200 works of art acquired by the Empress of Russia will illuminate her efforts to modernise Russian culture and to establish its capital as a centre of European art and life. And, as the AGO transforms itself the work of the renowned Canadian architect of the project will also be the subject of an exhibition, which will open in 2006. The showcase will include Frank Gehry's designs since creating the Guggenheim Museum in Bilbao, Spain.

One further highlight of a visit to the AGO is the **Henry Moore Sculpture Centre**, which is to remain open, it houses the world's largest public collection of this British artist's work. In a coup that most galleries can only dream about, the AGO was the recipient of a substantial part of a collection – including 139 bronzes and original plasters – donated by the sculptor. Moore worked closely with John C Parkin, the architect who designed the Sculpture Centre, and he insisted on overhead natural lighting. Without any doubt, it enhances the primeval feel of Moore's vast human figures, which continue to intrigue and captivate countless visitors to the gallery.

Despite being a work in progress for years to come the AGO is committed to making a visit here an essential stop for any art lover. At the end of your tour, allow time to wander around the gallery shop, with its enticing range of cards, prints, posters, books and numerous gifts.

Henry Moore Sculpture Centre

Ontario Place from the air

Option 7. Ontario Place

A 39-hectare (96-acre) waterfront park, Ontario Place is packed with activities for children, but also offers rewarding diversions for unencumbered adults.

–To the start: from the first weekend in May to the last weekend in September, a free shuttle bus service runs between Union Station and Ontario Place every 15 minutes.–

It is advisable to call ahead before visiting **Ontario Place** (955 Lakeshore Boulevard West, tel: 416-314-9900; daily 10am–8pm; www.ontarioplace.com). A Play All Day Pass® offers visitors unlimited use of most of the Ontario Place attractions and shows including the annual Canada Dry Festival of Fire and daytime Cinesphere films. A General Park Admission ticket is also available for access to the grounds only; parking and rides cost extra.

The dazzling white, geodesic dome stands out on the western end of Toronto's waterfront. Designed by Eberhard Zeidler, Ontario Place consists of three man-made islands connected by a series of bridges. From the main entrance, where the bus drops you off, it's a short walk, and you can also hire pushchairs for a minimal amount.

If you have children, you may as well head immediately to **Market Square** to check out the **Pre-School Kids Play** area, **Free**

Serious boating

Fall, which is just what it sounds like, and a ride not for the faint hearted, the mini-go karts at **Whiz Kids** and the **Mini Bumper Boats**. Nearby, also for younger kids, **Soak City** is a water play area, complete with shallow pools, fountains, spouts and Canada's tallest tipping bucket. It's sure to leave you drenched, but a good way to beat the heat. As Toronto's only water park,

Soak City features a good collection of water slides such as, **Pink Twister, Purple Pipeline** and **Hydrofuge**, a 70-degree slide down which people are hurled and twirled on an eighth of an inch sheet of water. This can keep kids happily and enthusiastically occupied for hours, especially on sweltering days. For those who prefer their fun dry, a little beyond the water park is **Treehouse Live! Stage**, an outdoor theatre that has children's entertainment daily.

If you continue along the waterfront towards the west you'll reach **Cinesphere** on the western end of Toronto's waterfront. This was the first permanent IMAX® theatre in the world, and it has a gigantic six-storey screen. Wherever you sit, you'll feel part of the action – which can be somewhat disconcerting, depending on the particular movie you're watching. A rotation of dramatic films focusing on subjects that lend themselves to absolutely stunning footage, from the majesty of nature to airborne acrobatics, starts at noon daily.

Go Zone, on the west island, is the place for older children. Be sure to check out the **Bumper Boats, Billy and Buster's Paddle Boat Adventure, H2O Generation Station** – the largest outdoor climbing structure of its kind in Canada – and **The Atom Blaster**, with its two levels of foam-ball fun. At the westernmost point of Ontario Place, **Adventure Island** has seven different mazes within **MegaMaze** that drive kids crazy and undoubtedly confuse their parents, while everyone is bound to have a soakingly good time on the flume called the **Wilderness Adventure Ride**, or have an outer space adventure on the **Mars** simulator ride.

With over 30 rides and attractions, and special events throughout the season, Ontario Place will keep the kids busy all day. Also, the operators of the park take the worry out of planning a trip, with their Guaranteed Weather programme. If it rains non-stop for an hour during park opening hours, and you've purchased a Play All Day Pass®, you can receive a voucher to come back any day during the season.

Cooling off

Although Ontario Place isn't known for its *haute cuisine*, there are plenty of snack bars and full-service dining rooms. A couple of them are based in the marina – which accommodates some 300 cruisers and yachts – and offer great waterfront views over Lake Ontario and the city, as well.

Also on site is a massive concert venue, the **Molson Amphitheatre**, which has 5,500 reserved seats under cover, 3,500 seats under the open sky and another 7,000 general admission seats on the lawn. An excellent sound-delay system allows those on the lawn to hear as well as people in the reserved seating, while two large video wall displays provide a closer view of the performers on stage. It's a delightful spot to spend a summer evening, listening to jazz, pop, blues or classical music. The concert ticket includes admission to Ontario Place, but not the price of parking or use of its attractions.

Option 8. Queen Street West and Environs

A neo-bohemian mecca in downtown Toronto, where the unexpected is the norm, both on the street and within the boutiques, bistros and book stores of Toronto's trendiest district. There is a wide choice of good restaurants; reservations are recommended for most of them.

–To the start: by TTC to Osgoode station.–

To get the most out of **Queen Street West**, start early in the evening to allow time for browsing before focusing on the evening's activities. As much as anything, people-watching is what makes Queen Street West so much fun. Many of the stores are open till 8pm, some even later. During the warmer months, folk-rock buskers and pavement artists swell the numbers on the street, as do some panhandlers. Don't be put off by the all-black uniform, shaved heads and pierced appendages of some of the trendier types – many of them students from the nearby Ontario College of Art – it's not *de rigueur*. An evening on Queen Street could be combined with a visit to either the **Royal Alexander Theatre** or the **Princess of Wales** (see *Day 1* for details and *Nightlife* section for phone numbers).

Soon after you set off west from University Avenue along Queen Street, you will become aware of the intriguing combination of new global merchandisers interspersed with such alternative lifestyle establishments as **The Condom Shack** (No 231) which sells around 40 different varieties, including mango and bubblegum-flavoured… to suit certain special tastes.

The cosy **Queen Mother Café** (No 208) is a landmark on the strip. Priding itself as Queen West's Grand Dame, it serves a Lao-Thai and pan-global menu. The intimate garden patio is a lovely place to relax on a warm afternoon or night.

Jazz and classical music buffs should investigate **Second Vinyl** at 2 McCaul Street. Next door, at No 4, **Native Stone Art** has been selling high quality handmade creations of native artisans for over 30 years. It has a wide variety of Inuit, Mohawk and West Coast cedar carvings that range in price from $25 to thousands of dollars. Here, you'll also find jewellery from the Navaho, Zuni and Hopi nations of the American southwest, as well as Cree moccasins and Cowichan sweaters.

The Friendly Stranger Cannabis Culture Shop (No 241) is an attractive shop that sells clothing made wholly or partially from hemp and a striking selection of hand-blown glass water pipes and other smoking accessories.

The **ChumCity Building** (No 299) is considerably more than a fine example of

Queen Street style

Street sounds

59

Black Bull Tavern

industrial Gothic architecture, partially adorned with rare terracotta tiles. This former headquarters of the United Church of Canada is now the command centre for CityTV, Space, MuchMusic and Bravo, several of the hottest TV channels in town. The entire building is wired up as a TV studio, and floor-to-ceiling windows allow passers by to witness live television at any time. A one-dollar donation to charity will automatically trigger the VideoBox to give you two minutes of airtime on **Speaker's Corner**, 24 hours a day. The wisest, wittiest, zaniest and most outrageous contributions are played back on CityTV each week.

Back on the north side of Queen, **El Mundo** (No 230) is a funky inexpensive gift shop with merchandise from all over the world, where you'll find ceramics from Japan and Morocco, amber originating in Poland that's set in silver from Thailand and beautiful sculptures from Indonesia. Stroll west to **Pages Books and Magazines** (No 256) to browse through its time-absorbing collection, which ranges from recent literature and old favourites to art and design, cultural theory and fetishism. They also have a good selection of small press Canadian books.

A stroll along Queen Street West

Throngs of Harley Davidsons are often parked outside the **Black Bull Tavern** (No 298), while their leather-clad owners quaff ale on the outside patio, but no one is intimidated. Beyond Beverley Street, the pavement on the north side of Queen widens and much impromptu street theatre takes place over the next few blocks. Be sure to check out the window of **Fashion Crimes** (No 322 1/2), where new clothing designed with a vintage look is sold. An eclectic combination of theatre presentations, poetry readings, alternative bands, a cosy martini bar and a stylish pool hall, as well as spicy Thai food, are guaranteed at **The Rivoli** (No 334; tel: 416-596-1908), while the superior offerings of the wine bar at **Le Select Bistro** (No 328, tel: 416-596-6405) ease the wait for an outside patio table and a chance to sample their delicious *prix fixe* menu.

As you approach Spadina Avenue you'll come to two rather different temples of culture: **David Mason Books** (No 342), which specialises in rare and out of print books, and the **Horseshoe Tavern** (No 368). The Horseshoe is an institution that has been verging on seedy since it began, but it has long been known as a forerunner in presenting talented musicians who have later become some of Canada's best musical acts – and it continues to draw important international acts.

Street stall bargains

Cross Queen Street and walk back along the south side past **Tortilla Flats** (No 429) for Tex-Mex cuisine. **Peter Pan** (No 373; tel: 416-593-0917) is a 1930s-style restaurant that serves a highly rated combination of Continental and Asian fare. Continuing east, drop by **Silver Snail** (No 367) if comic books are your hobby. The shop has a huge collection of collectibles, as well as a gaming section and a range of action figures. The **Bishop and the Belcher** (No 361) is a British-style pub with a good, wide selection of imported draft beers, while the Far East calls at **Sushi Time** (No 339, tel: 416-977-2222).

Turn right down John Street and enjoy the sensational up-close view of the CN Tower *(see pages 25–6)*. **Montana Bar and Grill** (No 145, tel: 416-595-5949) has good pub grub and prompt service, and you're unlikely to be disappointed by the creative menu at stylish **Avalon** (270 Adelaide Street West, tel: 416-979-9918), just around the corner. At King Street West, you can turn right and explore the possibilities of a glass of wine in the cacophonous bar of **Fred's Not Here** (321 King Street West, tel: 416-971-9155). Or turn left and head back through the glittering theatre block to the St Andrew subway station, located at the corner of King and University.

Excursions

Niagara

A full day, beginning with the 1¼ hour journey to Niagara Falls. There are coach tours from Toronto, but for maximum enjoyment, the trip should be done by car. In Niagara Falls, most attractions are open year round. Although the Shaw Festival in Niagara-on-the-Lake only runs from April to November, there's enough to enjoy in the off-season, particularly for history buffs. Phone ahead for theatre reservations, and book a table for lunch at the Queenston Heights Restaurant (April to January).

—To the start: drive to Niagara Falls from Toronto via the Queen Elizabeth Way (QEW freeway). Aim to leave by 8am. Follow signs to The Falls. When you reach the Niagara Parkway, turn right and park in the first parking lot with vacancies.—

The formation of the Niagara Escarpment began 450 million years ago when the forces of glacial action compressed ancient mountains into massive layers of rock and culminated in what is now one of the world's top tourist attractions, **Niagara Falls**. There will be no escaping the cloud of spray permanently hovering over the Falls once you join the **Niagara Parkway**, a 56-km (35-mile) route that extends the length of the Niagara River Gorge from Fort Erie to Niagara-on-the-Lake.

As you walk back towards the falls (if you've had to park far away, the People Mover will transport you up and down the Parkway all day, for the price of one ticket) look out for the memorial to Father Louis Hennepin, a Belgian missionary who was the chaplain on La Salle's Mississippi expedition in 1679. He supplied the first written record

Horseshoe Falls, Niagara

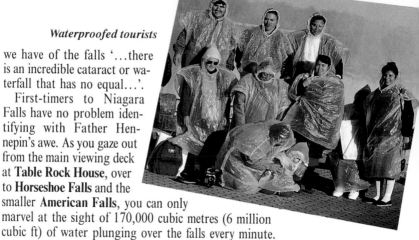

Waterproofed tourists

we have of the falls '…there is an incredible cataract or waterfall that has no equal…'.

First-timers to Niagara Falls have no problem identifying with Father Hennepin's awe. As you gaze out from the main viewing deck at **Table Rock House**, over to **Horseshoe Falls** and the smaller **American Falls**, you can only marvel at the sight of 170,000 cubic metres (6 million cubic ft) of water plunging over the falls every minute.

You may wish to have a quick cup of coffee at the fast food restaurant in Table Rock House. There's usually a lengthy queue for the **Table Rock Scenic Tunnels**. Carved between 1887 and 1902, they lead out to a portal right behind the falls. However, for a less claustrophobic and truly exhilarating adventure, continue along the Parkway to the complex that serves as base for the **Maid of the Mist** (tel: 905-358-5781), actually a fleet of small but sturdy boats that have been venturing into the basin of the falls since 1846. The trip will supply one of the most lasting memories of your holiday. Be prepared to get wet, despite the protection of the plastic raincoats (supplied). The daunting hubbub of the water as you get closer to the falls is nothing less than awesome.

You'll soon become aware that the town of Niagara Falls (dubbed 'the honeymoon capital of the world') is full of motels with heart-shaped beds and themed attractions such as **MarineLand**, **Ripley's Believe It or Not!**, the **Movieland Wax Museum**, the **FX Thrill Ride Theatre** and more, most of them on **Clifton Hill**. There's no time today, however, to investigate these any further, as you must return to your car.

Drive north up the Niagara Parkway towards Niagara-on-the-Lake. Back in 1943, Winston Churchill described the excursion as 'the prettiest Sunday afternoon drive in the world'. From the blossoming of the apple, cherry and peach trees in mid-May to the spectacular displays of fall foliage, it's always a glorious drive through the 1,254 hectares (3,100 acres) of immaculate parkland.

The **Niagara River Recreational Trail**, specifically created for pedestrians, joggers and cyclists, also winds its way between the road and the river. There are plenty of parking spots, and if you decide to follow the trail for a while, you're bound to pass some historical markers. The entire area was the scene of fierce and bloody battles during the War of 1812, after the United States first invaded Canada at Queenston, 11km (7 miles) to the north.

Continue along the Parkway, following signs to Queenston Heights, past the **Sir Adam Beck Generating Station**. Although the Niagara River is only 56km (35 miles) long, it drops a steep 99 metres (325ft), and its churning waters are one of the world's greatest

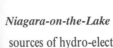

Niagara-on-the-Lake

sources of hydro-electric power. The turn-off to **Queenston Heights Park** and **Brock's Monument** is 1.5km (just under a mile) past the 15,000-plant **Floral Clock**. The view alone justifies lunch at the **Queenston Heights Restaurant** (tel: 905-262-4274). Perched on the edge of the Niagara Escarpment, the restaurant reigns over an unbeatable view of the lower Niagara River. Reservations are recommended, and the restaurant is closed from January to March. A Battle of Queenston Heights walking tour visits every major scene of the pivotal 1812 battle. You may also climb to the top of the 60-m (196-ft) monument commemorating General Isaac Brock, the British leader of the Canadian forces killed in the 1812–14 War.

As you continue towards Niagara-on-the-Lake, you will enter the heart of Ontario's wine country. Two well-known wineries, **Inniskillin** and **Rief**, have their own boutiques on the Parkway and offer tours. During the summer, stalls selling 'fresh tree-ripened fruit' line the Parkway.

Make a detour into the village of **Queenston**, site of the invasion by the United States troops in 1812. Canada's only operating Printing Museum can be visited in **Mackenzie House**, where William Lyon Mackenzie first published his strident views on reform in the *Colonial Advocate*, prior to the ill-fated Upper Canada Rebellion in Toronto in 1837.

Back on the Parkway, you'll get frequent glimpses of the river and pass more markers, such as the one at **Brown's Point**, where both

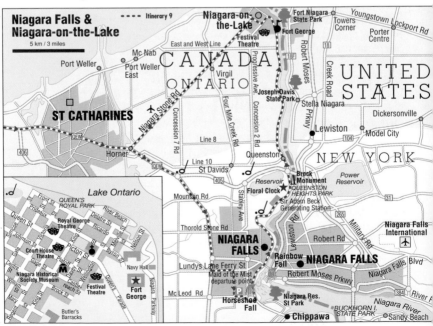

the Canadian York Militia and the American Army bivouacked on separate occasions during the War of 1812. **McFarland House** (open daily during the summer) was built in the early 1800s, and used as a hospital during the war by both British and American forces.

As you enter Niagara-on-the-Lake, **Fort George** (open early Apr–late Oct) is to your right, a reconstructed fort that was destroyed in 1812. Surrounded by wooden palisades, only the magazine of the original fortress remains, but commentary from costumed guides presents a vivid picture of early 19th-century garrison life.

Niagara-on-the-Lake is a delightful old town, first settled in 1780. The first five sessions of Upper Canada's legislature were held here under Lieutenant-Colonel John Graves Simcoe, between 1792 and 1796, when the town (then known as Newark) was the capital of Upper Canada. American forces captured it in May 1813, only to burn it down during their withdrawal the following December.

Feast fit for king

The **Shaw Festival Theatre** (tel: 1-800-511-7429) is world-renowned for its production of the works of George Bernard Shaw and his contemporaries. Each year the company presents 10 plays in three theatres, the **Festival**, the **Court House** and the **Royal George**.

Park your car – with luck you'll find a space on the main thoroughfare, **Queen Street** – and begin to explore. Most of the buildings have century-old shop fronts. One of the first you'll come to is the **Niagara Apothecary** at 5 Queen Street (mid-May–Labour Day, daily noon–6pm) which operated on this site from 1869 to 1960. Now a museum, its walnut cabinets and rows of antique ceramic storage jars show off the accoutrements of a Victorian pharmacy.

Queen Street and adjoining side roads offer shopping enthusiasts an assortment of stores to poke around in, from the long-established **Greaves Jams & Marmalades** (no preservatives, no advertising, non-stop business) to shops selling all kinds of collectibles, plus art galleries, boutiques, cafés and pubs. Consider eating at one of the local hostelries. You may like the Victorian elegance of the **Prince of Wales Hotel & Spa** (6 Picton Street, tel: 905-468-3246; www.vintageinns.com) or the dark wood and copper tables of the more informal **Buttery Theatre Restaurant** (19 Queen Street, tel: 905-468-2564).

Wander along the residential streets. Most homes were built within 20 years of the town fire in 1813. Time permitting, visit the **Niagara Historical Society Museum** (43 Castlereagh Street, tel: 905-468-3912; May–Oct daily 10am–5.30pm, Nov–Apr daily 1–5pm), before returning to Toronto, following signs to Highway 55, which joins Queen Elizabeth Way.

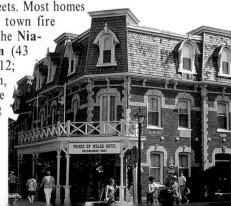

Prince of Wales Hotel

Shopping

Toronto has it all. Enormous shopping centres offering every conceivable type of store and service under one roof; residential neighbourhoods where old homes have been converted into speciality stores and boutiques; antiques markets and flea markets. From funky second-hand clothing stores to the most elegant of European fashions, from antiquarian books to New Age paraphernalia, the city is a shopper's dream. Most shops are open from 9 or 10am until 6pm, and often later, Monday to Saturday. The shops in the areas described below are all open on Sunday as well, although usually they don't open until noon.

The Toronto Eaton Centre

The Toronto Eaton Centre is a rhapsody to merchandising, with close to 300 stores and restaurants spread throughout five levels. It's the flagship location for many of the main fashion chains, such as **Banana Republic**, **Benetton**, **Esprit**, **Gap**, **Le Chateau** and **H&M**, but also houses nifty gift stores such as **Canadian Naturalist** and **Baskits**. You'll find jewellery and accessories, records and tapes, a variety of speciality shops (**Laco Sac** and **Silk & Satin**), a back rub salon, a foreign exchange centre, a fast jewellery and watch repair store, 30 fast food outlets featuring edibles from around the world, and seven full service restaurants such as **City Grill**, with its delightful view and patio overlooking Trinity Square. On the other side of Yonge Street in the **Jewellery Exchange** (215 Yonge Street) you will find more than 30 independent quality jewellers.

Queen's Quay Terminal

Over 30 shops reside in this speciality retail centre at the foot of York Street *(see Day 2, page 33)*. A very 1990s complex has been created within a historic lakeside building. Contemporary home furnishings, Canadian art

Toronto Eaton Centre

Harbourfront Antique Market

and craft, and contemporary fashions for men, women and children all have their place. **Amance Ladies Fashions** carries European and Canadian designs by Sharagano, Sinequanone, Steilmann and Susan Bristol. **Tilley Endurables** sells specially designed clothing for travel and adventure. Unique, handmade leather goods, can be found at **Roxalina**. Check out the art, craft and design by contemporary Canadian artists at **Proud Canadian Design** and **First Hand**. The store run by the **Arctic Nunavut** represents artists of the Canadian Arctic, featuring an exquisite range of handmade products. **Harris Gallery** also specialises in Inuit and Canadian sculptures. Look for treasures from around the globe at **International Marketplace** (June–Sept, weekends only), on the Waterfront Promenade.

Bloor to Yorkville

A large part of the action in Toronto's most elegant shopping zone takes place on and around Bloor Street between Yonge and Avenue Road. It's fun to browse, pricey to shop. There are some exceptions, such as **Science City** in the Holt Renfrew Centre, with an amazing assortment of scientific and educational gifts for children and adults. Right on Bloor Street is **Holt Renfrew**, popular with discerning matrons for many years. **Hazelton Lanes Shopping Centre** is possibly the zenith of shopping experiences. Women's and men's fashion boutiques include **Andrew's** and **Hugo Nicholson** for their exclusive evening wear, **Petra Karthaus** and TNT **Woman** for a variety of Europe's top designers. Canadian accessory designer's adornments are the focus at **Accessity**, while at **Lündstrom** you can see the clothes of Linda Lündstrom, a high profile Toronto designer. Other stores include **Nanni Belts & Designs** on Avenue Road and

Fashion and fripperies

Winston & Homes on Cumberland Street with its fine collection of pens. Every Toronto bride used to select her fine china from **William Ashley China**, which has the largest Waterford crystal selection outside Ireland. For First Nations and Inuit art, check out the **Guild Shop** on Cumberland. **Louis Wine** on Yorkville specialises in rare 18th-, 19th- and early 20th-century antiques, while **Paper Things** on Yorkville has quality cards, journals and personalised stationery – with all profits going to the National Ballet of Canada.

Mirvish Village

Mirvish Village and Honest Ed's

It's impossible to miss **Honest Ed's**, at the corner of Bloor and Bathurst *(see Day 3, page 35)*, with its ostentatious flashing sign of 22,000 light bulbs! Check out – probably briefly – the world-famous bargain shopping centre. People line up to get in, and 10 million visit it every year. There's no denying the bargains, and Ed Mirvish ensures that shopping is entertaining as well, through oodles of humorous signs. In considerable contrast, **Mirvish Village** on Markham Street offers tasteful antiques, folk art and vintage clothes shops. There's cinema memorabilia in **Vintage Video** and a world-class book store: **David Mirvish Books on Art**.

Yonge Street, north of Eglinton

Ten minutes by TTC from downtown, get off at Eglinton and walk north. Some would call the area North Toronto, and if you can tear yourself away from the fabulous shops and boutiques, there are some charming, residential side streets with solid older homes and a real sense of family. But first, the shops! For fashion stores with a unique stock, head to the **Casual Way**, **Mendocino** and **Higher Ground** (one for adults, one for children). Two family-owned shops are excellent – **Susanne Shoe Salon** for its wide-ranging inventory and **Just Cuz** with its buzz-worthy accessories. **Circle Shoes & Skate Exchange**'s selection ranges from Birkenstocks to Laurentian aboriginal boots and moccasins. Try **Jenny's Place**, for gifts of everything from jewellery to hair accessories to bags, hats and lovely underwear. Enjoy the intimate surroundings at BMV **Books**, as you browse through its new and rare books. Superb places to eat out include **Good Bite Restaurant**, a neighbourhood diner known for its tasty breakfasts, **Roberto's Ristorante Italiano**, with its chalkboard menu only, ensuring freshness, and **Centro Grill & Wine Bar** for a very special night out.

Queen Street West

This has been covered in *Pick & Mix Option 8, page 59*. If you decide to make it a daytime outing, you will find all the shops mentioned there, along with others such as **Aritzia** for hip women's clothing by West Coast designers and **Price Roman** for trendy tailored clothes.

Eating Out

Deciding where to eat in Toronto can be an onerous task, with over 4,000 restaurants to choose from. The waves of immigrants that have arrived in the city over the last hundred years from all parts of the globe have had a dramatic impact on the eating habits of the most WASP (an acronym for White Anglo-Saxon Protestant) of Torontonians.

There are few restaurants that specialise purely in Canadian cuisine, but a wide range of traditional Canadian foodstuffs and dishes make frequent appearances on menus – from Atlantic or British Colombian salmon to fiddleheads from New Brunswick, from Québec tortière to Canadian back bacon. And some of the excellent Canadian wines that have been acquiring top prizes at numerous international wine competitions are now appearing on the wine lists.

Stop for a snack

Besides the cuisines of the restaurants listed below, Torontonians can select from Argentinian, Armenian, Czech, Danish, Estonian, Ethiopian, Hungarian, Korean, Kosher, Mexican, Persian, Filipino, Somalienne or Sri Lankan fare – and much more besides.

The art of eating has risen to such heights that certain chefs, such as Greg Couillard, Jamie Kennedy, Mark McEwan and Susur Lee, are followed faithfully from restaurant to restaurant. Other diners pay homage to restaurant owners such as Franco Prevedello and Michael Carlevale, who between them have brought into being some of the finest Italian restaurants in the city – and Toronto has no shortage of excellent Italian restaurants.

The peak dining hour varies from restaurant to restaurant and area to area. It is best to check by phone first if you prefer to dine with the crowd, but want to be sure that you can guarantee a table. Reservations in advance are always advisable for the higher priced restaurants.

An approximate price guideline per person, excluding alcohol, taxes and tips is as follows: $ = under $30; $$ = under $50; $$$ = under $80; $$$$ = over $80.

Street eating

Asian

INDOCHINE
4 Collier Street
Tel: 416-922-5840
The Thai-Vietnamese menu includes six succulent crab preparations, crisp calamari and delicious noodle soups, touched with lemon grass and tamarind. A casual restaurant with colourful decor. *$$*

HIRO SUSHI
171 King Street East
Tel: 416-304-0550
This highly acclaimed Japanese sushi restaurant uses a variety of ingredient combinations, from traditional to avant-garde. Open from lunch to late night. *$$*

Jamaican hot spot

SEJONG
658 Bloor Street West
Tel: 416-535-5918
Its Japanese/Korean fare includes an elegant sushi bar, teriyaki, Korean barbecue and delectable tempura. Lots to eat and attentive service. *$$*

YOUNG THAILAND
81 Church Street
Tel: 416-368-1368
Popular Thai restaurant serving sophisticated, meticulously prepared food that comes with tiny pots of wonderful sauces: spicy, hot, tamarind, peanut, sweet and sour. A lively spot. *$$*

Canadian/American

AVALON
270 Adelaide Street West
Tel: 416-979-9918
A mix of subtle decor, excellent service and creative dishes by one of the city's leading chefs, Chris McDonald. A gastronomic delight. *$$$$*

BB33
33 Gerard Street West
Tel: 416-585-4319
Canadian cuisine served in two settings: a casual brasserie and an upmarket bistro. Try the pork tenderloin with apple walnut stuffing or the smoked caribou. *$$$*

CANOE
66 Wellington Street West
Tel: 416-364-0054
On the 54th floor of the TD Bank Tower, the menu includes innovative Canadian regional cuisine, with dishes such as roast hind of Yukon caribou. Popular with all kinds of foodies from Bay Street financiers to romancing couples. A fine view. *$$$$*

SENSES
318 Wellington Street West
Tel: 416-935-0400
At the SoHo Metropolitan Hotel, the innovative menu highlights the season's freshest ingredients. A tasting menu includes Saskatoon berry-rosemary shake, tea-smoked venison tenderloin and bee-pollen panna cotta. *$$$$*

Chinese

LAI WAH HEEN
108 Chestnut Street
Tel: 416-977-9899
Grand art deco eatery ensconced in the upmarket Metropolitan Hotel. Authentic ingredients, including numerous shark's fin and abalone dishes. Flawless *dim sum. Prix fix*e menus. *$$$*

Ripe and juicy peaches

LEE GARDEN
331 Spadina Avenue
Tel: 416-593-9524
Superb Cantonese dishes (check the daily specials) served amid lots of hullabaloo. A popular eatery with the locals in Chinatown. *$$*

Eclectic

KENSINGTON KITCHEN
124 Harbord Street
Tel: 416-961-3404
Delicious, mostly vegetarian Middle Eastern food. Leafy rooftop patio. *$$*

RODNEY'S OYSTER HOUSE
469 King Street West
Tel: 416-363-8105
A friendly   verging on raucous – basement restaurant, full of maritime paraphernalia. Few other places have the variety of live oysters, lobsters, crab and shrimp. *$$*

LE COMMENSAL FINE VEGETARIAN CUISINE
655 Bay Street
Tel: 416-596-9364
A delectable buffet with a wide selection of vegetarian food suitable for any diet. Pay by the weight. *$*

THE REAL JERK
709 Queen Street East
Tel: 416-463-6055
A real taste of Jamaica with its Bob Marley posters and colourful murals, jerk pork with rice and peas, cod fritters, boneless chicken roti, ginger beer and Caribbean-paced service. *$*

THE RED TOMATO
321 King Street West
Tel: 416-971-6626
A fun downtown spot for trendy uptowners. Visions of pink flamingos and veggies adorn the walls and the many zesty dishes include some cooked right at your table upon thick dolomite tiles heated in a 340°C/650°F oven. *$$*

SUPERMARKET
268 Augusta Avenue
Tel: 416-840-0501
A funky eatery in Kensington Market, with a globetrotting menu featuring dishes from Asia to the Caribbean, and speciality cocktails. *$*

French

BISTRO 990
990 Bay Street
Tel: 416-921-9990
Beloved bistro where French provincial fare is served in a farmhouse setting. Next best thing to a holiday. *$$$*

LE PARADIS
166 Bedford Road
Tel: 416-921-0995
Delightful authentic French bistro for those on a budget. Leave room for the homemade ice cream. Attracts actors, writers, producers and those who enjoy jazz in comfortable dining rooms. *$$*

Italian

GRANO
2035 Yonge Street
Tel: 416-440-1986
A touch of Italy with *faux* ancient-plaster walls, a garden, dining room

The splendid Splendido

and a party room. Where the connoisseurs of Italian congregate. *$$*

KIT KAT
297 King Street West
Tel: 416-977-4461
Authentic, home-style Italian food, served in various areas, under a very long solarium. Popular with media types and passing rock stars. *$$*

SPLENDIDO BAR & GRILL
88 Harbord Street
Tel: 416-927-7788
With colourful and zany decor, this is a place to be seen. Serving sumptuous dishes such as grilled sea bass or suckling pig roasted in a wood burning oven. *$$$*

International

BY THE WAY CAFÉ
400 Bloor Street West
Tel: 416-967-4295
A popular Annex eatery, with warm bohemian chic and a menu including dishes from Thailand to Mexico and the Mediterranean. *$*

THE DRAKE
1150 Queen Street West
Tel: 416-531-5042
In avant-garde West Queen West, the restaurant inside the hotel of the same name has a hip decor and challenging cuisine that highlights Asian, Latin and European flavours. *$$$*

JAMIE KENNEDY WINE BAR
9 Church Street
Tel: 416-362-1957
A casual 50-seat bistro, where the menu features inventive light tapas-style dishes – each with a wine selection – created by the well known chef. *$$*

NORTH 44°
2537 Yonge Street
Tel: 416-487-4897
Receiving constant rave reviews for its imaginative menu directed by Mark McEwan, this is a must for serious foodies. *$$$$*

Waiting for customers

SUSUR
601 King Street West
Tel: 416-603-2205
Susur Lee's East–West fusion has earned multi-star reviews. Seasonally themed seven-course tasting menus are served backwards, beginning with the main course. *$$$$*

TRUFFLES
21 Avenue Road
Tel: 416-928-7331
Award-winning French restaurant in the Four Seasons Hotel. Astute service of contemporary French cuisine in an elegant yet comfortable room. An intriguing wine list complements the many delectable dishes. *$$$$*

Nightlife

With over 180 theatre and dance companies, Toronto has the third-largest theatre industry in the English-speaking world, after London and New York. Besides blockbusters such as *The Lion King* and *Mamma Mia!*, theatre productions range from the traditional to the alternative.

Excellent Canadian works are produced by the Tarragon Theatre, Theatre Passe Muraille and Factory Theatre, while there's fun but thought-provoking theatre for children at Young People's Theatre. Buddies in Bad Times focuses largely, but not entirely, on gay and lesbian issues. Same day, discounted tickets for theatre and dance events can be purchased online at the TO TIX booth in Yonge-Dundas Square, at the southeast corner of Yonge Street and Dundas Street East (tel: 416-536-6468; Tues–Sat noon–6.30pm).

Music also flourishes: the Toronto Symphony Orchestra performs almost 10 months of the year in the Roy Thomson Hall, while the Canadian Opera Company and the National Ballet of Canada draw audiences to the Hummingbird Centre. The Four Seasons Centre for the Performing Arts – the first purpose-built opera house in Canada – will house both the opera and ballet companies. The Glenn Gould Studio, based in the Canadian Broadcasting Corporation headquarters, is a combined recording studio and public concert hall, designed principally for classical and jazz music. The Recital Hall, in the Toronto Centre for the Performing Arts, is also much acclaimed as a performance space.

Other options include a Tafelmusik concert – a Toronto-based, internationally renowned orchestra specialising in baroque music – or one of the regular poetry readings at the Idler pub.

Although Toronto's clubs are spread across the city, there are plenty of places to shimmy, line dance or simply rock.

For comprehensive listings on all performances and events, check either *Now* or *Eye*, free weekly newspapers available in many restaurants. Tickets for most events, including sporting events, can be purchased through Ticketmaster: contact

King Street West theatres

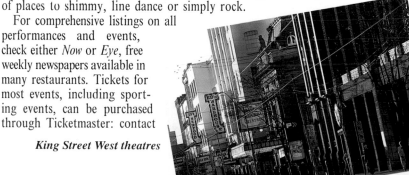

Skating at City Hall

them on tel: 416-870-8000, using a credit card. A service charge of $2–$5 is added to the ticket price.

Music

TORONTO CENTRE FOR THE PERFORMING ARTS
5040 Yonge Street
Tel: 416-733-9388

GLENN GOULD STUDIO
250 Front Street West
Tel: 416-205-5555

HUMMINGBIRD CENTRE
1 Front Street
Tel: 416-393-7458

MASSEY HALL
178 Victoria Street
Tel: 416-872-4255

ROY THOMSON HALL
60 Simcoe Street
Tel: 416-872-4255

Dance

PREMIERE DANCE THEATRE
207 Queen's Quay West
Tel: 416-973-4000

Theatre

BERKELEY STREET THEATRE
26 Berkeley Street
Tel: 416-368-3110

BUDDIES IN BAD TIMES THEATRE
12 Alexander Street
Tel: 416-975-8555

CANON THEATRE
244 Victoria Street
Tel: 416-364-4100

CANSTAGE
27 Front Street East
Tel: 416-368-3110

FACTORY THEATRE
125 Bathurst Street
Tel: 416-504-9971

PRINCESS OF WALES THEATRE
300 King Street West
Tel: 416-872-1212

ROYAL ALEXANDRA THEATRE
260 King Street West
Tel: 416-872-1212

ST LAWRENCE CENTRE FOR THE ARTS
27 Front Street East
Tel: 416-366-7723

TARRAGON THEATRE
30 Bridgman Avenue
Tel: 416-531-1827

THEATRE PASSE MURAILLE
16 Ryerson Avenue
Tel: 416-504-7529

Pubs, Clubs and Lounges

PANORAMA LOUNGE
55 Bloor Street West
Tel: 416-967-0000
The highest lounge in the city, on the 51st floor of the ManuLife Centre.

BLACK SWAN
154 Danforth Avenue
Tel: 416-469-0537
Live music every night, mainly blues.

C'EST WHAT
67 Front Street East
Tel: 416-867-9499
A comfortable brew/vin pub and

restaurant with live indie music from local bands.

CHICK 'N' DELI
744 Mount Pleasant Road
Tel: 416-489-3363
A neighbourhood bar with great ambience and cheap food, classic rock on week nights, jazz and Dixie weekends.

THE DOCKS
11 Polson Street
Tel: 416-469-5655
Possibly Canada's largest patio party under the sun and stars, with three options for the club-goer – the Deep End Nightclub, Tides and the intimate Aqua Lounge.

EL CONVENTO RICO
750 College Street
Tel: 416-588-7800
Latino reigns! A multi-ethnic crowd comes for the salsa, merengue and disco. Drag queen shows on Friday and Saturday nights.

THE EMBASSY
223 Augusta Avenue
Tel: 416-591-1132
A down-to-earth, yet chic, resto-lounge in Kensington Market, where music runs from Afrobeat to ska to indie.

FREE TIMES CAFÉ
320 College Street
Tel: 416-967-1078
A cosy bistro with live folk and acoustic entertainment nightly that has been drawing the crowds for over 20 years.

THE GLADSTONE
1214 Queen Street West
Tel: 416-531-4635
In Toronto's oldest continuously operating hotel, three bars – The Ballroom, the Melody Bar and the Art Bar – with karaoke, cabaret, film screenings and book launches.

A bite with a beat

GUVERNMENT
132 Queen's Quay East
Tel: 416-869-0045
A waterfront hot spot, with disco and live rock 'n' roll.

HORSESHOE TAVERN
370 Queen Street West
Tel: 416-598-4753
The classic rock 'n' roll bar that's been dishing up great blues, rock and alternative live music from bands across the country and beyond for over 50 years.

JOKER
318 Richmond Street West
Tel: 416-598-1313
A megaclub spread over three floors, dishing up 1980s retro, hip-hop and R&B. Great views over the city.

MADISON AVENUE PUB
14 Madison Avenue
Tel: 416-927-1722
A popular watering hole with students and the Anglo/Irish crowd.

MONTREAL BISTRO & JAZZ CLUB
65 Sherbourne Street
Tel: 416-363-0179
Nightly sets of modern, New Orleans and traditional jazz.

ALWAYS IN GOOD TASTE
Chick 'n' Deli
TAKE OUT 489-9464
VIRGIL SCOTT
NEXT CHUCK JACKSON
MON CHUCK JACKSON

Outdoor nightlife

OASIS
294 College Street
Tel: 416-975-0845
Toronto's smallest concert hall. Live music; state-of-the-art sound system.

PHOENIX CONCERT THEATRE
410 Sherbourne Street
Tel: 416-323-1251
Two huge dance rooms: DJs play rock, alternative, rock 'n' roll and disco.

REX JAZZ AND BLUES BAR
194 Queen Street West
Tel: 416-598-2475
At the forefront of the city's jazz scene. A Downtown Jazz Festival venue.

SECOND CITY
99 Blue Jays Way
Tel: 416-343-0011
Live revue comedy and theatre. Dinner/theatre packages available.

VINNIE'S SOCIAL HALL TORONTO
22 Duncan Street
Tel: 416-979-5565
A vast space, much of it occupied by televisions, pool tables and video games.

YUK YUK'S COMEDY CABARET
224 Richmond Street West
Tel: 416-967-6425
Stand-up comedy Tuesday to Sunday.

Gay Scene

BAR 501
501 Church Street
Tel: 416-944-3272
A casual watering hole with pinball machines, TVs and pool tables.

BYZANTIUM
499 Church Street
Tel: 416-922-3859
A chic dining room with an adjoining bar renowned for its martinis. From jazz to classics to house music.

FLY
8 Gloucester Street
Tel: 416-410-5426
Hugely popular club, with frequent line-ups. Two chill-out lounges downstairs and a cavernous dance space upstairs. DJs play tribal and circuit music.

PEGASUS BAR
491 Church Street
416-927-8832
A convivial hangout, with a few local gay-friendly straights. Billiard tables, dartboards; a place to relax after work.

WOODY'S AND SAILORS
Tel: 467 Church Street
Tel: 416-972-0887
This popular and well-run gay bar is renowned for its theme nights.

Calendar of Special Events

All public holidays are marked with an asterisk.

JANUARY / FEBRUARY

New Year's Day*
Toronto International Boat Show (mid-January): attracts serious and wannabe nautical enthusiasts.

Canadian International Auto Show (mid-February): the latest in automotive trends and technology. www.autoshow.ca.

WinterCity Festival (late-January/ early February): a two-week citywide culinary festival; free entertainment.

MARCH / APRIL

Toronto Sportsmen's Show (mid-March): targets the hunting and fishing brigade. www.sportsmensshows.com.

One of a Kind Show and Sale (late March, early April): a vast range of uniquely handcrafted items are displayed. www.oneofakindshow.com.

Good Friday* and **Easter Sunday*** (between late March, and mid April)

Toronto Blue Jays take up residence at Rogers Centre for the upcoming American League baseball season.

MAY

International Children's Festival (mid-May): performers from around the world. www.harbourfront.on.ca.

Santé – The Bloor-Yorkville Wine Festival (mid-May): a five-day festival attended by international winemakers and some of the city's top chefs.

Victoria Day* (officially the Monday preceding May 25)

JUNE

Toronto International Festival Caravan (mid-June): a week-long celebration during which the cuisine and culture of Toronto's ethnic communities are experienced in over 40 pavilions. www.caravan-org.com.

Pride Week – Toronto (mid-June): the largest lesbian and gay pride event in North America, culminating in a

A Blue Jay hero

Beaches Jazz Festival

street fair, festival and a parade. Tel: 416-927-7433; www.pridetoronto.com.

Queen's Plate (last Saturday): the oldest stakes race in North America, held at the Woodbine Race Track.

Toronto Downtown Jazz Festival (last week): a 10-day festival featuring over 500 Canadian and international musicians at free concerts as well as at ticketed galas. www.torontojazz.com

Toronto Argonauts: return to the Rogers Centre for the football season.

JULY

Canada Day* (July 1): day-long celebrations at Harbourfront Centre and Nathan Phillips Square.

CHIN Radio Station Picnic (first weekend): sponsored by the local Italian radio station, it's a gigantic, three-day funfest on Toronto Island.

The Fringe of Toronto Theatre Festival (first 10 days): avant-garde works are performed in the Annex neighbourhood by almost 80 theatrical companies and over 400 performers from around the world. Tel: 416-966-1062; www.fringetoronto.com.

Molson Indy Toronto (middle weekend): attracts the world's racing superstars. www.molsonindy.com.

Toronto Outdoor Art Exhibition (mid-July): an annual art festival that features works by artists from across Canada, the US and Europe. www.torontooutdoorart.org.

Caribana (last week): a Mardi Gras-like 10-day celebration of the Caribbean spirit, highlighted by a street parade of 5,000 celebrants dressed in dazzling costumes. www.caribana.com.

Beaches International Jazz Festival (last weekend): an annual musical gathering in the Kew Gardens Bandshell, and along Queen Street East from Woodbine to Beech. www.beachesjazz.com.

AUGUST

Civic Holiday* (first Monday)

Canadian National Exhibition (mid-

Celebrating Caribana

Flying high at CNE

equestrian season. A 10-day event with animals, and competitions. www.royalfair.org.

Christmas Past in Historic Houses (mid-November to mid-January): The Toronto Historical Board opens Colborne Lodge, Mackenzie House and Spadina, to recreate a Dickensian, Victorian and Edwardian Christmas respectively.

Canadian Aboriginal Festival (end of November): North America's largest multi-arts aboriginal event at Rogers

August to Labour Day weekend): One of the world's most popular annual fairs, with exhibitions, live music, and amusement for children. www.theex.com.

SEPTEMBER

Labour Day* (first Monday)

Toronto International Film Festival (second week): the second-largest film festival in the world. Stars and cinematographers celebrate the world of cinema. www.bell.ca/filmfest.

Word On The Street (last Sunday): crowds jam Queen Street West during this annual book and magazine fair and authors read from their new fall titles. www.thewordonthestreet.com.

OCTOBER

Thanksgiving Day* (second Monday)

International Festival of Authors (middle week): major cultural event. Worldwide writers give nightly readings from their work, at Harbourfront Centre. www.readings.org.

Toronto Raptors: the city's NBA (basketball) team takes to the court at the Air Canada Centre. www.raptors.com.

Toronto Maple Leafs: ice hockey resumes at the Air Canada Centre. www.mapleleafs.com.

NOVEMBER

Royal Agricultural Winter Fair (mid-November): the world's largest indoor fair. It incorporates the Royal Horse Show, which is the highlight of Canada's

Royal Agricultural Fair

Centre presents music awards, a large craft market and traditional foods.

One of a Kind Show and Sale (late November/early December): a 10-day fair with rare Christmas gifts from over 500 Canadian craftspeople and artists.

Cavalcade of Lights (last Friday): a family affair, as the city's Christmas lights are switched on by the mayor, and professional ice skaters thrill the crowds in Nathan Phillips Square. www.toronto.ca/special_events.

DECEMBER

Christmas Day* (25th)
Boxing Day* (26th)
First Night Toronto – New Year's Eve (31st): a family-oriented, alcohol-free multicultural festival in the Distillery District. www.firstnighttoronto.com

PRACTICAL information

GETTING THERE

By Air

Toronto's Lester B Pearson International Airport is on the northwest corner of

Pearson International Terminal

Toronto, 32km (18 miles) from the downtown core. Since the opening of Terminal 3 in 1991, the airport has been linked by more than 35 airlines to major American and international destinations. Pearson is currently undergoing a redevelopment programme that includes the replacement of Terminals 1 and 2 with a single terminal. Terminal 1 currently handles Air Canada and Air Canada Jazz domestic and international flights. In 2006 Terminal 2 will be phased out and its operations switched to the expanded Terminal 1. Check which terminal you will fly in to and out of. For flight information: tel: 416-247-7678.

Pacific Western provides an Airport Express bus service (tel: 905-564-6333; www.torontoairportexpress.com) every 20 to 30 minutes, to seven downtown hotels and the bus terminal (approximately $16 one way, $27 round trip). The service operates between 4am and 1am (the following day). Allow 1–1½ hours for the journey, depending on traffic and the weather.

There are separate taxi and limousine stands at the arrivals level of each terminal. Only taxis with TIA on their license plates are authorized to pick up passengers from Pearson International Airport, and the fare to the centre of the city is approximately $40. The limousine services, with their larger cars and uniformed drivers, charge a set fee, which is usually in the $45–50 range.

Toronto is also served by the Toronto Island Airport, which handles short-haul commuter flights. Located in the main harbour area, it's a brief ferry ride to the foot of Bathurst Street, and a very short taxi ride to the downtown core.

By Rail

VIA **Rail**, in conjunction with **Amtrak**, operates passenger rail services from Union Station, connecting Toronto to cities across Canada and within the United States. Although there is not much cost difference between train and air tickets (depending on the season, or the day of the week), rail travel offers a more relaxed way of viewing the countryside, and the train deposits you right in the heart of Toronto. For information about train travel with either company, tel: 416-366-8411.

By Road

If you are driving up from New York State, the Queen Elizabeth Way is the main highway to Toronto. Highway 401, which crosses the city's northern reaches, extends from Windsor (3 hours) and Michigan in the west, to Montréal (5½ hours) in the east (once within Québec, it becomes Highway 20). Highway 401 is North America's second busiest highway, with first place going to the San Diego Freeway. As a result, the police strictly enforce the speed limit on various sections of the highway. Signs for distances and speed limits are shown in kilometres, with the speed limit of 100km/h (60mph) on highways, 60km/h (35mph) in the city. None of the aforementioned highways are particularly scenic, but they are fast, and there are numerous fast food restaurants and filling stations with attractive picnic areas behind in which to stretch your legs. Note that the use of seat belts is mandatory in Ontario, under provincial law.

By Bus

The main bus terminal is at 610 Bay Street, at the corner of Bay and Dundas Streets, very close to City Hall and Eaton Centre. It is the base for Greyhound Lines of Canada (tel: 416-393-7911), a national company that offers scheduled services from across the country and links into the Greyhound system within the United States, and several other bus companies.

TRAVEL ESSENTIALS

Visas & Passports

Foreign visitors, including those from the UK and from countries other than the United States, must have a valid passport to enter Canada. US citizens must carry a passport or a birth certificate, along with photo ID, and naturalised Americans must have naturalisation certificates with photo ID. Permanent residents of the US require the alien-registration card.

Children travelling without both parents must have notarised authorisation from the absent parent, or they will be refused entry. Also, anyone with a criminal conviction (even for a minor traffic offence) could be refused entry, so consult the Canadian Embassy in your home country before making travel plans.

Visitors of any nationality planning to stay over three months in Canada may require a visa. For more information, refer to Citizenship and Immigration Canada: www.cic.gc.ca, or tel: 1-800-242-2100.

By Ferry

When the Toronto–Rochester, New York, fast ferry service is running passengers can

Winter transport

make the trip across Lake Ontario from Rochester in New York State to Toronto Harbour in 2½ hours. For information about schedules and ticket prices tel: 877-283-7327; www.nfl-bay.com.

Customs

Visitors from America or overseas who are at least 19 years old are allowed to bring in 1.14 litres of liquor, 1.5 litres of wine or up to 24 bottles or cans (355 ml/12oz each) of beer, and gifts not exceeding $60. Duty and tax has to be paid on the balance if the gifts are worth over $60. Anyone over 19 years old may bring in 200 cigarettes, 400gms (14oz) of tobacco and 50 cigars. There are also restrictions on importing meats, dairy products and agricultural products. A rabies certificate must be presented by the owners if a pet is brought into Canada. For further information call Canada Customs, tel: 1-800-461-9999 within Canada or 506-636-5064 from outside the country; www.cba.gc.ca

Ready to glide

Weather

Toronto's location on the north shore of Lake Ontario ensures a reasonably temperate climate, particularly compared with the rest of Ontario, which suffers considerably harsher winters. The lake acts as a coolant during the summer, yet keeps the city warmer during the winter. Summers are fairly dry and warm (average temperature: (+23°C/73°F), winters are cool with a minimum of snow (-6°/21°F). Spring (+6°C/42°F) and fall (+10°C/50°F) can be most pleasant, with sunny days and cooler nights. For an up-to-date forecast on weather in the Toronto area, tel: 416-661-0123. For out-of-town weather, tel: 416-661-0082. From elsewhere in Canada, you may call 1-900-565-5000, which costs 95 cents per minute.

Clothing

Much depends on the time of year you plan to visit. If you come during the winter, heavy warm coats, gloves and boots are essential. Being a cosmopolitan city, very little raises eyebrows these days. However, since walking is one of the best ways to get to know the city, bring comfortable footwear. During the daytime, casual wear is perfectly acceptable. Concert-going or dining at some of Toronto's smarter restaurants, require more formal dress. During the heat of the summer, when most buildings are air-conditioned, it's a good idea to have a light jacket or sweater to put on. Likewise, during the winter months, buildings are kept extremely warm (by British and European standards, at least) and it is not necessary to wear layers of thick sweaters – unless you like to roast!

Electricity

Standard 110 voltage is used in Canada, the same system as in the United States. Visitors from the US do not need to bring electrical adapters or converters.

GETTING ACQUAINTED
Geography and Population

Toronto is on the northern shore of Lake Ontario, 558km (348miles) west of Montreal, 131km (81miles) from Niagara Falls, Ontario, 154km (95miles) from Buffalo, New York and 378 km (235 miles) from the Windsor/Detroit area. Between road, rail, water (through the Port of Toronto) and air, the city is well-connected to all parts of the province, the continent and the world.

One of Toronto's charms is that despite being one of the world's fastest growing cities, it still has a much treasured system of ravines that criss-cross the city, providing a wilderness of sorts for the 4.8 million people who inhabit the Greater Toronto Area. Indeed, Toronto is the largest city in Canada, with 15 percent of the country's 30 million population. In 1989 the United Nations deemed it the world's most ethnically diverse city. The influence of the immigrants and refugees on Toronto has, over the years, created a vibrant, cosmopolitan city.

MONEY MATTERS

Although there is no limit to the amount of money a visitor can bring into Canada, technology in the banking field has virtually eradicated the need to bring in huge sums. Any bank or exchange house can change foreign currency for Canadian funds, and many stores, hotels and restaurants accept American currency. Most downtown banks are open from either 8am–4pm or 9am–5pm, and there are cash machines on almost every corner. Major credit cards are also accepted at most establishments.

Travellers' cheques are one of the safest ways of carrying money abroad. If lost or stolen, American Express Travellers' cheques can be replaced within 24 hours, sometimes by courier. Transactions are simplest if the cheques are in Canadian funds.

Taxes

Welcome to the land of confusion. A provincial sales tax of 8 percent is levied on goods and services. Prices displayed in shops, restaurants and hotels do not include the tax. Visitors can apply for a refund under the Canada Tax Back Program provided they have accumulated over $200 worth of original receipts for non-disposable merchandise to be used outside Ontario. For information on this refund, as well as for a refund of the 5 percent accommodation sales tax that is charged by all hotels, tel: 1-800-268-3736.

The Goods and Services Tax (GST) of 7 percent is charged on most goods and services sold in Canada. Visitors can claim a rebate of the GST paid on short-term accommodation of less than a month, and on most goods they have bought to take home with them. To qualify for a refund,

Bilingual signpost

the purchase amount of each receipt must be at least CAN $50. Warning: refund desks at hotels and airports charge a fee to process the claim. For information: tel: 1-800-668-4748 (in Canada), or 902-432-5608 (outside Canada).

Tipping

In restaurants the service charge is rarely included in the bill and the usual tip is 15 percent. Still under discussion since the introduction of the GST is whether the tip should be on the total of the bill, or on the pre-tax total. The final decision rests with the customer, and often depends on the size of the bill. Taxis and limousine drivers usually get a 10–15 percent tip, hotel porters expect at least 50 cents per bag and room service is $1 per day per person. Tips in American currency are particularly gratefully received.

Trolley in a hurry

GETTING AROUND

Public Transit

The Toronto Transit System (TTC) is an excellent public transit system, that is clean, safe and inexpensive. Its underground subway trains connect with above-ground buses and street cars to provide a vast network covering the city. A transfer ticket enables you to switch from the subway to a bus or street car and there is a considerable saving if you buy 10 at once. The Blue Night Network operates a safe mode of transport after dark.

There are also two Day Passes, each priced at approximately $8. The first is good for one person, for unlimited travel after 9.30am Monday to Friday to 5.30am the following morning, and from 6am on Saturday. The second – and this is an amazing bargain – is for up to two adults and four children or one adult and four children or youths on Sundays and holidays. There are three main lines a U-shaped north–south line, one east–west line, with a connection from Union Station down to Harbourfront via the Harbourfront LRT, and the Sheppard line, running east from Yonge to Don Mills. For full details on fares and routes, pick up the Ride Guide from the subway collectors' booths, call TTC Information, tel: 416-393-4636 or visit: www.toronto.ca/ttc.

GO Transit operates a regular bus and train service that connects suburban areas to various TTC stations and downtown, tel: 416-869-3200 or 1-888-438-6646; www.gotransit.com.

Car Rental

Driving a car around Toronto is fairly straightforward provided you have a good map that marks the one-way streets and someone to navigate. However, parking

is expensive, especially during the day, and street parking can be difficult to find.

Most of the major car rental companies have offices at the airport, and downtown. Some of the main companies are:

Alamo Rent A Car tel: 1-800-327-9633
Avis Rent A Car tel: 1-800-879-2847
Budget Rent A Car tel: 1-800-561-1212
Discount Car and Truck Rentals tel: 1-800-263-2355
Dollar Rent A Car tel: 1-800-800-4000
Hertz tel: 1-800-263-0600
National Car Rental Canada tel: 1-800-387-4747
Thrifty Car Rental tel: 1-800-367-2277.

Tours

Special interest tours are available, although not all of them operate year-round: Heritage Toronto Walking Tours, tel: 416-338-0684; A Taste of the World Neighbourhood Bicycle Tours & Walks Inc, tel: 416-925-0554; www.TorontoWalksBikes.com; Genova Tours, tel: 416-367-0380.

Taxis

Except in the middle of a snow storm, it is usually easy to hail a cab, certainly in the downtown area. There are also taxi stands outside the main hotels, Union Station, and dotted throughout the financial core of the city. Drivers are not allowed to pick up two fares unless a customer advises the driver to pick up the second one. The largest taxi companies are:

Beck Taxi tel: 416-751-5555
Co-op Cabs tel: 416-504-2667
Diamond tel: 416-366-6753
Metro Cab tel: 416-504-8294.

Underground City

There's practically a separate city underneath downtown – a 10km (6 mile) network known as PATH, which extends six blocks north from Front Street to Dundas Street and five blocks west, from Yonge Street over to John Street. It can be entered from any of the downtown subway stations, several of the main hotels and some larger office complexes. The shops below ground are as varied as those above, and during any extremes of climate the Underground City provides instant relief.

HOURS AND HOLIDAYS

Business Hours

Most offices are open from 9am–5pm, although as flexi-hour work schedules gain in popularity, many open earlier. Government offices are usually open from 8.30am–5pm, and the main downtown Post Office at 31 Adelaide Street East is open 8am–5.45pm, Monday to Friday. The main downtown stores open at 10am (although closing hours vary from 6pm to 9pm Monday to Friday). Weekend hours are usually Saturday 9am–9pm, Sunday noon–5pm. The Eaton Centre is open Monday to Friday 10am–9pm, Saturday 9am–9pm, Sunday noon–5pm.

ACCOMMODATION

Since most of the tours suggested here are in and around downtown Toronto, the hotels recommended are all in the downtown area. There is accommodation to match every budget. Although the rates quoted are for the lowest rate for a standard double room, do enquire about special packages and promotions when making reservations. All hotel rates are subject to 5 percent sales tax, 7 percent Goods & Services Tax and a 3 percent levy for marketing the city. (Unfortunately, there are two other unavoidable taxes – an 8 percent tax on food and a 10 percent tax on alcohol.)

Bed & Breakfast is a popular option in Toronto. Many of the homes are in residential neighbourhoods, with hosts who are delighted to share their knowledge of the city. The price for two is usually in the $75–$125 range, including parking.

The prices for the hotels have been categorised as follows: $ = under $100; $$ = 100–150; $$$ = 150–200; $$$$ = over $200. All prices are in Canadian dollars and all are correct at the time of going to press, but do check when making bookings, as they may have changed.

DELTA CHELSEA HOTEL (1,590 rooms)
33 Gerrard Street West
Tel: 416-595-1975 / 1-800-243-5732
Fax: 416-585-4393
www.deltachelsea.com
Just steps from Yonge Street, the Eaton Centre and other downtown attractions. Specialising in programmes for children, including a Children's Creative Centre. *$$$*

FOUR SEASONS HOTEL TORONTO
(380 rooms)
21 Avenue Road
Tel: 416-964-0411 / 1-800-268-6282
(Canada), 1-800-332-3442 (US)
Fax: 416-964-2301
www.fourseasons.com
Part of the international Four Seasons group, this is a multi-award-winner in the heart of Yorkville. Spacious bedrooms and marble bathrooms; a twice-daily maid service and a high staff-to-guest ratio ensure personalised service. *$$$$*

HILTON TORONTO (601 rooms)
145 Richmond Street West
Tel: 416-869-3456 / 1-800-267-2281
Fax: 416-869-3187
www.hilton.com
Comfortable, business-oriented hotel in the heart of downtown's shopping district, within walking distance of the Art Gallery of Toronto and theatres. *$$$$*

HOLIDAY INN ON KING (425 rooms)
370 King Street West
Tel: 416-599-4000 / 1-800-263-6364
Fax: 416-599-4785
www.hiok.com
Steps from the theatre district and the Metro Toronto Convention Centre, marble and mahogany are the urbane theme of this business hotel. Views of Lake Ontario and Rogers Centre from some rooms. *$$$*

INTERCONTINENTAL TORONTO CENTRE
(586 rooms)
225 Front Street West
Tel. 416-597-1400 / 1-800-422-7969
Fax: 416-597-8128
www.torontocentre.intercontinental.com
A 25-storey tower adjacent to the Metro Toronto Convention Centre. Geared towards business travellers. The high glass walls and ceiling of its Azure Restaurant

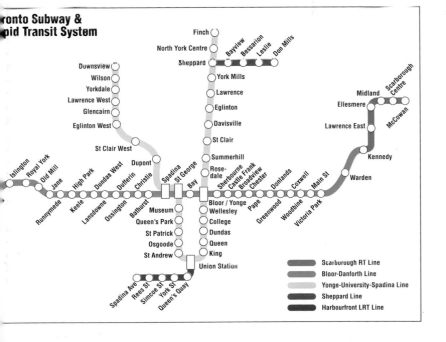

Family homes offer B&B

and lounge provide a memorable setting for watching falling snow. *$$$$*

INTERCONTINENTAL YORKVILLE TORONTO (210 rooms)
220 Bloor Street West
Tel: 416-960-5200 / 1-800-267-0010
Fax: 416-960-8269
www.interconti.com
Wood panelling, gleaming brass and touches of art deco in the lobby. Luxurious rooms with windows that open, and a courtyard. Close to the Royal Ontario Museum. *$$$$*

HOTEL LE GERMAIN (122 rooms)
30 Mercer Street
Tel: 416-345-9500 / 1-866-345-9501
Fax: 416-345-9501
www.hotelboutique.com
A sleek and luxurious boutique hotel, with helpful staff, in the heart of the Entertainment District. Acclaimed restaurant, Luce, has excellent regional Italian dishes. *$$$$*

LE ROYAL MERIDIEN KING EDWARD HOTEL (294 rooms)
37 King Street East
Tel: 416-863-3131 / 1-800-543-4300
Fax: 416-367-5515
www.lemeridien-kingedward.com

Edwardian landmark that has graced the Toronto scene since 1903; its vaulted ceilings, marble pillars and opulent public rooms have been elegantly restored. *$$$$*

NOVOTEL TORONTO CENTRE (262 rooms)
45 The Esplanade
Tel: 416-367-8900 / 1-800-NOVOTEL
Fax: 416-360-8285
www.accorhotels.com
A comfortable European-style hotel that's part of a French chain, within minutes of the St Lawrence Market, the financial district, shopping and major entertainment venues. *$$$*

PANTAGES SUITES HOTEL AND SPA (111 rooms)
200 Victoria Street
Tel: 416-945-5444 / 1-866-852-1777
Fax: 416-214-5618
www.pantageshotel.com
One of Toronto's newest boutique and lifestyle hotels in the heart of downtown Toronto, close to Massey Hall, the Canon Theatre and the Eaton Centre. *$$$$*

PARK HYATT TORONTO (346 rooms)
4 Avenue Road
Tel: 416-925-1234 / 1-800-977-4197
Fax: 416-924-6693
www.parktoronto.hyatt.com
Restored Toronto landmark in a prime location on the corner of Avenue Road and Bloor, close to fashionable Yorkville and two minutes from Royal Ontario Museum. Its 18th-floor Roof Lounge has long been a favourite with the literati. *$$$$*

RADISSON ADMIRAL – TORONTO HARBOURFRONT (157 rooms)
249 Queen's Quay West
Tel: 416-203-3333/1-800-333-3333
Fax: 416-203-3100
www.radisson.com/toronto_admiral
Intimate hotel on the busy waterfront. Polished brass, lacquered wood and marine art emphasise a nautical theme. *$$$*

THE FAIRMONT ROYAL YORK
(1,365 rooms)
100 Front Street West
Tel: 416-368-2511/1-800-441-1414
(Canada and US)
Fax: 416-368-9040
www.fairmont.com
This elegant hotel, built in 1929, continues to symbolise tradition, starting in the comfortable lobby with its gleaming chandeliers, fresh flower arrangements and invitingly plump armchairs. *$$$$*

SHERATON CENTRE TORONTO
(1,377 rooms)
123 Queen Street West
Tel: 416-361-1000/1-800-325-3535
Fax: 416-947-4874
www.sheratontoronto.com
With over 60 boutiques and access to the 10-km (6-mile) Underground City. Amenities include the city's largest swimming pool and a rambling landscaped garden. Rooms have excellent views of the city. *$$$$*

SOHO METROPOLITAN HOTEL (88 rooms)
318 Wellington Street West
Tel: 416-599-8800
Fax: 416-599-8801
www.soho.metropolitan.com
A luxurious boutique hotel with high-tech rooms, within a condominium complex that has a spa and Senses Restaurant. *$$$$*

TORONTO MARRIOTT EATON CENTRE
(459 rooms)
525 Bay Street
Tel: 416-597-9200/1-800-228-9290
Fax: 416-597-9211
www.marriotteatoncentre.com
Perfect location for shoppers, as the hotel is connected to the Eaton Centre. An indoor rooftop pool offers a different view of the city. *$$$$*

WESTIN HARBOUR CASTLE (977 rooms)
1 Harbour Square
Tel: 416-869-1600/1-800-228-3000
Fax: 416-869-1420
www.westin.com/harbourcastle
All rooms have views over Lake Ontario or the city. It has a relaxed atmosphere,

Guardians of the law

even though it's just a step away from the financial centre. Spectacular views from the 38th-floor Toula Restaurant and Bar. *$$*

Bed and Breakfast

Three registries representing B&B homes in the downtown area will supply brochures on request. They are: **Bed and Breakfast Homes of Toronto**, tel: 416-363-6362, www.bbht.ca; **Bed & Breakfast Association of Downtown Toronto**, PO Box 190, Station B, Toronto, Ontario M5T 2W1, tel: 416-410-3938/1-888-559-5515, fax: 416-483-8822, www.torontobedandbreakfast.com; and **Toronto Guild of Bed and Breakfasts**, 241 Seaton Street, Toronto, Ontario M5A 2T5, tel: 416-925-3061, fax: 416-925-2522, www.torontoguild.com.

HEALTH AND EMERGENCIES

For emergencies requiring the police, an ambulance or the fire service, tel: 911. All non-Canadian visitors should purchase health insurance before leaving home. The following numbers may be useful.
Canadian Medic Alert: tel: 416-696-0267
Dental Emergency Service: tel: 416-485-7121 (8am–midnight)
Telehealth Ontario: tel: 1-866-797-0000 (24-hour advice freephone; registered nurse).
Manulife Health: tel: 1-800-COVERME; www.coverme.com

Hockey Hall of Fame

Credit Cards (lost or stolen):
Amex Canada: tel: 1-800-221-7282 for lost or stolen travellers' cheques
Diners Club: tel: 1-800-363-3333
Mastercard: tel: 416-232-8020
Visa: 1-800-847-2911.

COMMUNICATIONS AND NEWS

Telephone

Two area codes, 647 and 289, have been added to the previous Toronto area codes of 416 and 905. Now the entire 10-digit number must be dialled for any number within Toronto. The 1-800 and 1-877 numbers are toll-free if dialled from within Canada. Some numbers within area code 905 and 289 are considered a local call, others are long distance. If you are calling a long distance number, dial 1 first; if it is not a long distance call, you simply dial 905 or 289 and the rest of the number. The long distance information pages at the front of the telephone directory provide further information. If unsure, call the operator on 0. To find a number anywhere in Canada, tel: 411 or visit: www.canada411.ca. Local calls made from a phone box are charged at standard rate, no matter how long they may be.

Media

Toronto has four daily English-language newspapers, *The Globe and Mail* and *The National Post* (both circulated nationally), *The Toronto Star* and *The Toronto Sun*. The two major consumer magazines are *Maclean's*, a weekly news magazine, and the 10 times a year *Saturday Night*. National and regional radio and television stations are based in Toronto, including the Canadian Broadcasting Company (CBC), which operates nation-wide networks in French and English for both radio and television, and CTV. Toronto has two alternative newspapers, *Now* and *Eye*, which provide comprehensive, up-to-date listings.

USEFUL INFORMATION

Attractions

Toronto has myriad museums. *Black Creek Pioneer Village*, on the northwest outskirts of Toronto, is a re-created village in which visitors can stroll through Ontario's past. *The Toronto Historical Board* operates a number of historic homes that are open to the public, as well as *Old Fort York*, a recreation of the original settlement. *The Hockey Hall of Fame* is situated on the concourse level of BCE Place – although part of the collection is in the old (1885) Bank of Montréal building at the corner of Front and Yonge. The *Toronto Zoo* is a long trek out, in the Rouge Valley of Scarborough, but well worth the effort. You needn't be deterred by the weather as many of the animals are in huge pavilions such as the Indo-Malayan Pavilion or the African Pavilion. In winter, cross-country skiers combine a tour of the zoo with visits to the pavilions to warm up!

People with Disabilities

An excellent publication, *Toronto With Ease*, is produced by Tourism Toronto, in partnership with Disability Today. The annual publication covers lodging, attractions, dining, hospitals, places of worship and transport. It can be ordered by calling 1-800-363-1990.

SPORT

Whatever the season, there is always a sporting event to attend. During the winter, the Toronto Maple Leafs, who are in the National Hockey League (ice hockey) and the basketball team, the Toronto Raptors, both play before enthusiastic crowds at the Air Canada Centre. During the spring, summer and autumn, the Toronto Blue Jays, who are part of the American League, bring baseball to Rogers Centre, and the Toronto Argonauts, play a Canadian-style football also at Rogers Centre. For those more actively inclined, there's the Martin

Goodman Trail, a 22-km (13-mile) jogging and cycling path beside Lake Ontario. In winter, skaters can take a spin on the rink at Nathan Phillips Square or at Harbourfront Centre's York Quay.

USEFUL ADDRESSES

Tourist Offices

TOURISM TORONTO
Suite 590, Box 126
207 Queen's Quay West
M5J 1A7
Tel: 416-203-2600/1-800-363-1990;
Fax: 416-203-6753;
www.torontotourism.com
Operating a toll-free line providing information on places to stay and things to do. Monday to Friday 8.30am–6pm, Saturday 9am–5pm, Sunday 10am–5pm (summer only), tel: 416-203-2600 for local calls, 1-800-363-1990 for calls from Ontario, Greater Montreal and the US.

They also have a stand in the Ontario Travel Information Centre in the Atrium on Bay, 20 Dundas Street West, on the ground floor.

Embassies

CONSULATE GENERAL OF THE UNITED STATES
360 University Avenue (north of Queen Street), M5G 1S4
Tel: 416-595-1700

BRITISH CONSULATE-GENERAL
777 Bay Street (corner of College Street), Suite 2800, M5G 2G2
Tel: 416-593-1290

FURTHER READING

Discovering Ontario's Wine Country by Linda Bramble & Shari Darling, Stoddart Publishing Co Limited, 1992.
The Estates of Old Toronto by Liz Lundel, Boston Mills Press, 1997.
The French Side of Toronto by Franco Toronto Media & Publishing, 2004.
Great Country Walks Around Toronto by Elliot Katz, Great North Books, 1993.
Insight Guide: Canada, Apa Publications 2005; *Insight Guide: Montreal*, Apa Publications 2005.
Old Toronto Houses by Tom Cruikshank, Firefly Books Ltd, 2003.
The Other Guide to Toronto: Opening the Door to Green Tourism by the Green Tourism Association, 2000.
Toronto Architecture – A City Guide by Patricia McHugh, McClelland & Stewart Inc, 1989.
The Toronto Story by Claire Mackay & Johnny Wales, Annick Press Limited, 1990.
Toronto Street Names: An Illustrated Guide to their Origins by Leonard Wise and Allan Gould, Firefly Books, 2000.
Toronto: A Literary Guide by Greg Gatenby, McArthur & Company, 1999.

Boating on the ice

Index

ACKNOWLEDGMENTS

Photography	Ottmar Bierwagen *and*
10	Archive Canada
13	Canadian National Exhibition Archives
11	Sutro Library
12	Toronto Historical Board
14	Toronto Transit Commission
33B	Martha Ellen Zenfell
Front Cover	Trevor Varley/Alamy
Back Cover	Ottmar Bierwagen
Handwriting	V.Barl
Cover Design	Klaus Geisler
Cartography	Berndtson & Berndtson

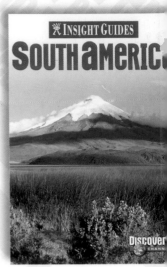

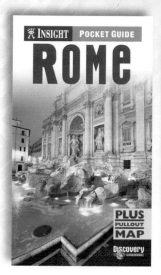
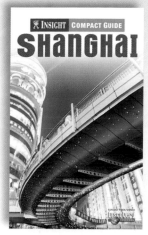

☀ INSIGHT GUIDES

The World Leader in Visual Travel Guides & Maps

As travellers become ever more discriminating, Insight Guides is using the vast experience gained over three-and-a-half decades of guidebook publishing to create an even wider range of titles to serve them. For those who want the big picture, Insight Guides and Insight City Guides provide comprehensive coverage of a destination. Insight Pocket Guides supply personal recommendations for a short stay. Insight Compact Guides are attractively portable. Insight FlexiMaps are both rugged and easy to use. And specialist titles cover shopping, eating out, and museums and galleries. Wherever you're going, our writers and photographers have already been there – more than once.

NOTES